501 WORLD CUP MOMENTS

The  Report

Love great sportswriting? So do we.

Every month, Pitch Publishing brings together the best of our world through our monthly newsletter — a space for readers, writers and fans to connect over the books, people and moments that make sport so captivating.

You'll find previews of new releases, extracts from our latest titles, behind-the-scenes interviews with authors and the occasional giveaway or competition thrown in for good measure.

We also dip into our back catalogue to unearth forgotten gems and celebrate timeless tales that shaped sporting culture.

Scan the **QR code** and join the growing Pitch Publishing reader community today.

Luciano Wernicke

501 WORLD CUP MOMENTS

Stars, Teams, Goals and Curiosities from Football's Greatest Show on Earth

First published by Pitch Publishing, 2026
1

Pitch Publishing
9 Donnington Park, 85 Birdham Road
Chichester, West Sussex, PO20 7AJ
www.pitchpublishing.co.uk
info@pitchpublishing.co.uk

© 2026, Luciano Wernicke

The moral right of the author and illustrator has been asserted in accordance with the Copyright, Designs and Patents Act 1988

Every effort has been made to trace the copyright.
Any oversight will be rectified in future editions at the earliest opportunity by the publisher.

No part of this book may be used or reproduced in any manner for the purpose of training artificial intelligence technologies or systems. In accordance with Article 4(3) of the DSM Directive 2019/790, Pitch Publishing expressly reserves this work from the text and data mining exception.

Set in Adobe Caslon 10.3/15pt

Typeset by Pitch Publishing

Cover design by Olner Design

Printed and bound in India by Replika Press Pvt. Ltd.

The authorised representative in the EEA is
Easy Access System Europe OÜ, Mustamäe tee 50, 10621 Tallinn, Estonia gpsr.requests@easproject.com

A CIP catalogue record for this book is available from the British Library

ISBN 978-1-83680-419-2

Papers used by Pitch Publishing are from
well-managed forests and other responsible sources

Contents

Preface	9
The Road to the World Cup	11
Uruguay 1930	17
Italy 1934	27
France 1938	37
Brazil 1950	46
Switzerland 1954	55
Sweden 1958	66
Chile 1962	76
England 1966	86
Mexico 1970	96
West Germany 1974	103
Argentina 1978	113
Spain 1982	122
Mexico 1986	130
Italy 1990	139
United States 1994	149
France 1998	159
South Korea and Japan 2002	168
Germany 2006	178
South Africa 2010	188
Brazil 2014	198
Russia 2018	206
Qatar 2022	214

To Nadia, who is still lighting my way.

Preface

THE WORLD Cup is humanity's most important tournament; no other sporting event inspires such passion among people on every continent. According to FIFA, the 2022 World Cup in Qatar attracted five billion fans across all media – linear television, digital media, social media, and streaming platforms – and the final between Argentina and France had an audience of 1.42 billion viewers. Huge numbers reflect the passionate enthusiasm the competition inspires.

This book offers an exciting journey through almost a century of football history, but its title is a little bit of a fraud: here, dear reader, you will not find 500 exciting moments from the World Cup. If you count the articles one by one, you will discover that there are many more. This doesn't mean that I'm bad at maths. Well, yes, I failed some courses in school, but the numerical licence is for another reason. The vast history of the number one tournament in sports is so rich in joys, sorrows, controversies, records and curiosities that its glimpses forced me to go far beyond 500 stories.

For almost a century, since the inaugural edition in Uruguay in 1930, the World Cup has offered diverse stages on which artists, madmen, and criminals – as the brilliant author Osvaldo Soriano would say – have performed. In the following pages, you'll find a tasty selection of gems that, I'm sure, will satisfy your appetite for epics starring real-life champions and villains, even if they seem straight out of the chronicles of Herodotus – or Marvel comics. I hope you enjoy it.

Luciano Wernicke
Buenos Aires

The Road to the World Cup

* Football was born in England. Although ball games – with or without the use of hands – existed among various ancient peoples (in present-day China, Japan, Greece, and Italy, among others), it was in the United Kingdom that the pastime became a sport with the drafting of the first rules and the invention of the leather ball with an inflatable rubber bladder inside. The first version of the code now considered official was drafted in a London pub called the Freemasons' Tavern, which no longer exists. There, a group of representatives from various clubs created the Football Association, the world's first entity dedicated to regulating football, and it was also there that they wrote the first rules of what would become the most popular sport of all time.

* The most curious aspect of the original statute is that the pitch was to be almost 200 metres long, the goals consisted of two posts separated by eight yards (7.32 metres) without a crossbar, and neither the number of players per team nor the length of the matches were specified.

* The rules evolved. In 1866, a friendly match between two teams from London and Sheffield determined that football squads should have 11 players, and matches should last for 90 minutes, divided into two 45-minute halves. Over the years, the figure of a referee appeared, and the crossbar for the goals was

eight feet high (2.44 metres). In 1871, the Football Association Challenge Cup – commonly known as the FA Cup – was established in England, the oldest official tournament currently held worldwide.

* On 5 March 1870, a match between national teams was played in London: England and Scotland drew 1-1 at Kennington Oval, a venue originally created for cricket. This inaugural game, however, is not considered legitimate by some sports historians because the 11 'visiting' footballers lived in the British capital and, moreover, had not been selected by the Scottish Football Association.

* 'Whatever the Scotch 11 may have been composed the right to play was open to every Scotchman whether his lines were cast north or south of the Tweed. The fault lies on the heads of the players of the north, not on the management who sought the services of all alike impartially. To call the team "London Scotchmen" contributes nothing. The match was, as announced, to all intents and purposes between England and Scotland.' This was a complaint by English Football Association secretary Charles Alcock that the match that inaugurated international games was not deemed 'official' by his colleagues in Glasgow.

* According to records, the first official match between two national teams took place on 30 November 1872, on a pitch belonging to the West of Scotland Cricket Club, located in the Partick neighbourhood on the outskirts of Glasgow. On that day, in front of barely 3,000 spectators, Scotland – made up of players from a single club, Queen's Park FC, and wearing blue, the team's alternative uniform – and England drew 0-0.

THE ROAD TO THE WORLD CUP

* Twelve years later, in 1884, the British Home Championship emerged, the first competition designed for national teams, in which England, Scotland, Wales, and Ireland participated. The 1900 Paris Olympic Games opened the door to football, which had been absent four years earlier in Athens, the first tournament of the modern Olympic era. Only three clubs participated in the French capital, representing their respective countries: Club Français of France, Université de Bruxelles of Belgium, and Upton Park FC of England, who won the tournament.

* Outside the United Kingdom, the first international match took place in 1885, when Canada defeated the United States 1-0 in Newark, New Jersey. This game is also not considered 'official' because the visitors represented the Western Ontario Football Association, and the hosts the now-defunct American Football Association, an organisation that, despite its name, was only regional in scope – the United States Soccer Federation, the first national institution, was not founded until 5 April 1913. Various journalistic investigations claim that the first international match played outside Great Britain, supported by the respective national associations, was played on 20 June 1902 in Montevideo, between Uruguay and Argentina: the visitors won 6-0.

* On 21 May 1904, delegates from the football federations of France, Belgium, Denmark, the Netherlands, Spain, Sweden and Switzerland founded the Fédération Internationale de Football Association (FIFA) in Paris. The English Football Association, chaired by Scotsman Lord Arthur

Kinnaird, refused to send a representative. At its inaugural session, some bylaws were approved, which contemplated the unification of regulations based on those in use at the time in Great Britain – the promotion of the sport, and efforts to incorporate other countries. At that meeting, work also began on the idea of a competition between national teams for 1905 or 1906: groups were drawn up, and the possibility of Switzerland hosting the semi-finals and final was even considered, but the initiative failed due to financial difficulties.

* After the Swiss proposal evaporated, the Olympic Games became the main venue for football tournaments for national teams. The first edition with countries' squads was London 1908, which featured five sides: Great Britain, France, Denmark, Sweden and the Netherlands. Little by little, the tournament added competitors from other continents: in Antwerp 1920, Egypt was the first African country to participate. In Paris 1924, the United States and Uruguay were the first from the Americas.

* Uruguay won the gold medal in 1924 in Paris and repeated that success four years later, in Amsterdam. These achievements demonstrated that football was no longer the exclusive preserve of Europeans.

* On 8 September 1928, in Zurich, FIFA delegates – which had already incorporated England, Scotland, Austria, Italy, Hungary, Czechoslovakia, Norway, Canada, the United States, Argentina, Uruguay and Chile, among others, as affiliated nations – agreed that the inaugural edition of the World Cup would be held in July 1930.

THE ROAD TO THE WORLD CUP

* On 18 May 1929, during a FIFA Congress developed beneath the Gothic arches of the Saló de la Reina Regent in Barcelona City Hall, five nations expressed their will to host the inaugural World Cup: Italy, Sweden, the Netherlands, Hungary and Uruguay. The South American country was chosen by 46 delegates from 23 countries based on two essential reasons: sporting, linked to its double Olympic championship in 1924 and 1928; and financial, because the Uruguayan delegate, Enrique Buero, assured that the Uruguayan Football Association would cover all travel and accommodation costs for the delegations, something the representatives from the Old World were unable to meet. At the Barcelona Congress, it was also agreed that the international competition would be held every four years, and that the host of the next edition would be a European country. The history of the World Cup had finally begun.

Statistical focus – all World Cup winners:

Brazil	5 (1958, 1962, 1970, 1994, 2002)
Italy	4 (1934, 1938, 1982, 2006)
Germany/West Germany	4 (1954, 1974, 1990, 2014)
Argentina	3 (1978, 1986, 2022)
Uruguay	2 (1930, 1950)
France	2 (1998, 2018)
England	1 (1966)
Spain	1 (2010)

Uruguay 1930

* The first edition of the World Cup took place between 13 and 30 July 1930, in Montevideo, the capital city of Uruguay. For this significant tournament, the local government decided to build a large stadium with a capacity for 70,000 spectators where all the matches would be played. However, due to a storm that lasted for several days, the construction could not be finished on time and the first games were played on the fields of the Nacional and Peñarol clubs. Uruguay 1930 is the World Cup in which the fewest stadiums were used: only three. In addition, it is the only one in which all the matches took place in a single city.

* The designation of Uruguay as the first World Cup venue discouraged the participation of many European teams. Countries like England, Spain, Italy, Hungary, the Netherlands and Germany, among others, refused to compete. Some national associations blamed economic problems, others said that the clubs had refused to release their players for almost two months: in addition to their stay in the small South American nation to participate in the tournament, the players had to cross the Atlantic Ocean by boat, a journey that at that time took about two weeks to go and another two to return. Although the Uruguayan Soccer Association (AUF, the acronym in Spanish for the Asociación Uruguaya de Fútbol) agreed to pay the travel and lodging expenses

of the delegations, only four teams arrived at the port of Montevideo from Europe: those from France, Belgium, Yugoslavia and Romania. The rest of the participants – Argentina, Brazil, Chile, Bolivia, Paraguay, Peru, Mexico and the United States – arrived from North and South America. Without teams from Asia, Africa and Oceania, the World Cup in Uruguay was attended by only 13 teams, the equal smallest number of participants in history along with that of Brazil 1950. Given such a low attendance, it was not necessary to hold a qualifying round to reach the tournament.

* Due to the meagre presence of participating countries, the organisers decided to form three groups of three teams, plus another of four, which after the draw was made up of Argentina, Mexico, Chile and France. The winners of each group went directly to the semi-finals.

* The coach of the French team, Gaston Barreau, worked as secretary of the National Conservatory of Music in Paris. Although Barreau insisted on being allowed to travel with the team to Uruguay, the authorities of that institution refused: they considered it excessive for him to be absent from his post for the required two months. Barreau, who managed France in 197 matches, had his revenge in 1938 when he was able to lead *Les Bleus* in a World Cup.

* The FIFA president, French lawyer Jules Rimet, travelled with his country's team and a very special passenger: the World Cup. Created by sculptor Abel Lafleur, the trophy consisted of a small chalice held by a female figure representing the Greek goddess of victory, Nike. The work, 55cm high, weighing

four kilograms and costing 50,000 francs, was cast in 18-carat gold and mounted on a base of semi-precious stones. Rimet disembarked in Montevideo on 5 July and, the next day, handed the cup to the president of the AUF, Raúl Jude, who immediately deposited it in the vault of the República bank, to be kept safe until the end of the championship.

* The competition regulations indicated that the team that won the tournament would keep the trophy until the next World Cup, when it had to be returned to FIFA. Also, the first country to win the World Cup three times would retain the prize for ever. In 1970, in Mexico, Brazil won their third World Cup and took the valuable trophy, which by then was already known as the Jules Rimet Trophy in honour of the competition's original promoter. In 1983 it was stolen from the headquarters of the Brazilian Football Confederation in Rio de Janeiro. The thieves melted it down to produce small gold ingots, which they then sold to jewellery manufacturers.

* After arriving in Montevideo, the Mexican squad held its first training session on a field located on the grounds of the Salesian school, Pío IX. For the second, they had to move to another property because the priests in charge of the school complained to the organising committee about the large number of swear words used by the team's Spanish coach, José Juan Luqué de Serrallonga, to yell at his players when they made a mistake.

* For this first edition, FIFA had decided that all matches would be played with balls made in Argentina. But, after a protest by the Uruguayan Minister of Industry, it was agreed that locally made

balls would also be used. They were similar: made in leather, dark brown, with rectangular sections and an outer seam. The Uruguayan ones were slightly larger. The organising committee arranged for the captains of the two teams to choose which ball to play with before the start of the matches. Except in the games in which Uruguay participated, in all the others the players preferred the Argentine balls.

* Before the World Cup began, the famous tango singer Carlos Gardel visited the hotels where the Uruguayan and Argentine teams were staying and gave recitals to entertain the players.

* The first World Cup began on 13 July 1930 with two matches. Mexico and France faced each other at the Estadio de los Pocitos – the Peñarol stadium, which was later demolished in 1940 – and the United States played against Belgium at Parque Central, the home of Nacional. According to the newspapers of the time, the duel between the Aztecs and the French started eight minutes earlier, which is why it is considered the first of the 964 World Cup matches played over 22 editions of the tournament up to and including Qatar 2022. The reports agree in pointing to the Frenchman André Maschinot as the person responsible for kicking the ball for the very first time in the most important sporting event in the world.

* The French forward Lucien Laurent was the scorer of the first of the 2,720 goals netted over the 22 editions of the World Cup. Laurent, who was employed by the Peugeot car company, beat Mexican goalkeeper Óscar Bonfiglio in the 19th minute with a right-footed volley.

URUGUAY 1930

* 'In those days, soccer players did not kiss each other after each goal,' said Lucien Laurent of his historic goal and how it was celebrated.

* In the 23rd minute between Mexico and France, when the score was 1-0 to the Europeans, goalkeeper Alex Thépot collided with Mexican forward Dionisio Mejía and ended up unconscious on the field. Thépot was taken off the pitch and transferred to a hospital, where he was treated by doctors. Since substitutions were not allowed at that time, France continued with ten men and with the goal defended by midfielder Augustin Chantrel. Despite the mishap, France won 4-1. Chantrel's performance was highly praised by the media at the time.

* The regulations of the 1930 World Cup indicated that the rest periods between the two halves of a match should be 'five minutes minimum, and 15 minutes maximum, according to the referee's decision'. Shortly after, FIFA would determine that the recess would be 15 minutes in all official matches.

* On 14 July, Romania defeated Peru 3-1 at Peñarol's field. This match was witnessed by just over 300 spectators, the smallest attendance in the entire history of the World Cup.

* In that match, Romanian forward Adalbert Steiner suffered an injury after a collision with Mario de las Casas. The situation caused a fight between both sets of players, which according to the official FIFA report ended with the expulsion of Peru's Plácido Galindo, the first player to be sent off a pitch in a World Cup. The sanction by Chilean referee Alberto Warnken was 'verbal', because the yellow and red cards used to caution or expel

players would not be used in the World Cup until 1970 in Mexico.

* Argentine forward Manuel Ferreira played in his team's 1-0 victory over France on 15 July at Parque Central, but not in their second match, against Mexico. Why? In addition to playing football, Ferreira was studying at university to become a public notary and on the same day of the game against the Mexicans, 19 July, he had to take an exam in Buenos Aires. The proximity of the capitals of Argentina and Uruguay, separated by the wide Río de la Plata river, allowed the forward to return to his country and, the following day, rejoin the squad.

* On 16 July, Chile were leading Mexico 1-0. Six minutes into the second half, Mexican defender Manuel Rosas Sánchez – a young amateur player who worked professionally as a baker – scored the second goal of the match, but for Chile: in an attempt to deflect the ball, Rosas Sánchez accidentally put it into the Mexican net. That unfortunate action became the first own goal in the history of the World Cup.

* The match in which Yugoslavia beat Bolivia 4-0, on 17 July at Parque Central, was refereed by Uruguayan Francisco Mateucci, who at 27 years and 62 days old became the youngest referee in the annals of the World Cup.

* Also that day, the United States beat Paraguay 3-0. Their three goals were scored by Bertrand 'Bert' Patenaude, a striker born in Fall River, Massachusetts, who played only four games for his country and scored six goals: four in the 1930 World Cup and two against Brazil in a friendly played in

URUGUAY 1930

Rio de Janeiro after the tournament, on 17 August, which ended 4-3 to the home team.

* The stadium built especially for the World Cup finally hosted a match when, on 18 July, Uruguay defeated Peru 1-0. The date of this inaugural game is not a coincidence: it also marked the first century of Uruguayan independence. That is why the stadium was named the Estadio Centenario.

* The French goalkeeper Alex Thépot was the first to save a penalty in the World Cup. On 19 July, at the Estadio Centenario, Thépot saved from Chile's Carlos Vidal. His feat was not enough to prevent his team from losing 1-0.

* Following Chile's victory against France, Argentina beat Mexico 6-3 in the same stadium. Mexico goalkeeper Óscar Bonfiglio saved another penalty, from Fernando Paternoster, then Argentine stopper Ángel Bossio also kept out a spotkick, from Manuel Rosas. In that match, Bolivian referee Ulises Saucedo – who was also the coach of his country's national team – awarded three penalties: two for Mexico (from the second, Manuel Rosas had his revenge and scored the first World Cup goal from the spot) and one for Argentina. This record has never been surpassed in the competition, and only equalled in Austria v Hungary in Italy in 1934 and in the final of Qatar 2022, in which, coincidentally, Argentina also played.

* During the semi-final between Argentina and the United States, played 26 on July at the Estadio Centenario, the coach of the American team, Bob Millar, entered the field to assist one of his players, James Brown, who had been injured. Millar went

on to the pitch with a suitcase full of oils, ointments and medicines and, upon opening it, a small bottle containing chloroform fell out. The jar lost its cork, spilled its contents on the grass, and the trainer, when trying to retrieve the bottle, breathed in the chloroform vapours and fainted. Millar had to be removed from the field by his own players. Brown, meanwhile, recovered on his own, without any treatment, and continued playing. Argentina won 6-1.

* In the other semi-final, Uruguay defeated Yugoslavia by the same score. The Europeans had opened the scoring after four minutes, but Uruguay led 3-1 before the end of the first half. According to newspaper reports, the third goal came from a free kick that was headed off the pitch, but the ball bounced off a policeman standing next to the touchline – one version even states that the officer went on to the pitch to stop the ball from going out – and remained in play, without the Brazilian referee Gilberto de Almeida Rêgo or his linesmen, the Bolivian Ulises Saucedo and the Frenchman Thomas Balvay, noticing. The action continued and the ball ended up in the Yugoslav net. The Balkan players vehemently protested the goal, which was nevertheless awarded by De Almeida Rêgo. Uruguay crowned their victory with three more goals and qualified for the final. The Yugoslavs, meanwhile, were so angry at what they considered an injustice that they did not show up to play the match for third place with the United States. It remains the only game in the entire history of the World Cup in which one of the contenders was absent.

URUGUAY 1930

* Belgian Jan Langenus had two jobs during the World Cup in Uruguay: as a referee, he took part in four matches; as a journalist, he acted as a correspondent for the German magazine *Kicker* throughout the tournament. After each game, Langenus passed a report by telephone to a colleague in the publication's office.

* The final of the first World Cup was played on Wednesday, 30 July 1930, at the Estadio Centenario, between Uruguay and Argentina. As the captains of the two teams – José Nasazzi and Manuel Ferreira – could not agree on which ball to use, Jan Langenus decided that the one made in Argentina would be used for the first half, and the Uruguayan one for the second. The first half ended with Argentina leading 2-1; in the second, Uruguay overcame the disadvantage with goals from José Cea, Victoriano Santos Iriarte and Héctor Castro and won 4-2. Castro was nicknamed *Manco* (one-armed) because he had lost his right hand in an accident with an electric saw when he was 13.

* 'They beat us by being more brave and more clever, not by being better players,' said Argentine striker Francisco Varallo, analysing that final many years later.

* After the final, the organisers called the champions together to raise the Uruguayan emblem on the flagpole and present them with the World Cup, but at that moment they noticed that the president of the AUF, Raúl Jude, had forgotten to remove the trophy from the vault of the República bank. To save embarrassment, someone got a replacement trophy and gave it to the scorer of the first goal in the final,

Pablo Dorado. As a result, the winning team did the lap of honour with a fake cup instead of the official prize.

* The first world champions received their medals – almost four months after the final had finished! In addition, the Uruguayan Football Association only awarded the prizes to the 11 men who had played in the final. Peregrín Anselmo, Pedro Petrone, Santos Urdinarán and Domingo Tejera, who had participated in other matches prior to the duel with Argentina, did not receive anything, the same as the seven other players who completed the official squad list of 22.

Statistical focus – teams with the most World Cup appearances:

Team	Appearances
Brazil	22†
Germany	20
Argentina	18
Italy	18
Mexico	17

†Only Brazil have played in every World Cup

Italy 1934

* In October 1932, a FIFA Congress held in Stockholm, Sweden, awarded Italy the right to host the 1934 World Cup. Several delegates complained that, at the time, the chosen country was ruled by dictator Benito Mussolini, leader of the National Fascist Party. They feared that he would use the tournament as a means of propaganda for his regime and that he would bribe referees to pave the way for the *Azzurri* to win the title.

* For this second edition, the competition was modified: the initial round with groups was discarded and a direct elimination stage was adopted, starting from the round of 16. This dizzying format resulted in eight of the 16 participating nations being eliminated in their first match.

* The 1934 World Cup attracted 32 entries, thus establishing a preliminary competition phase for the first time: 21 European nations competed for 12 spots; four from South America for two; four from North America and the Caribbean for one; and three from Asia and Africa competed for the last spot, which went to Egypt.

* Uruguay refused to participate. According to some newspaper reports, the reason for their absence was that, after the inauguration of the professional era in 1932, many clubs did not want to release their players for the two months required by the round-

trip boat journey to Europe and the stay in Italy. Another, and probably more accurate, explanation states that Uruguay decided to repay the rejection of many teams from the Old World, including Italy, from the 1930 tournament. In one way or another, the sky-blue squad became the only champions not to defend their title in the following tournament.

* The first World Cup qualifying match was played on 11 June 1933, at Råsunda Stadium in Solna, north-west of Stockholm: Sweden thrashed Estonia 6-2. This game also saw the first substitution in an official FIFA-approved game: Arnold Laasner replaced Friedrich Karm for the Estonians. Although substitutions were not permitted by the regulations, for this first qualifying round, FIFA agreed that, for each match, the managers of the two teams would agree on the possibility of replacing the goalkeeper in case of injury, as well as one or two of the outfield players.

* On the afternoon of 25 February 1934, at Dalymount Park in Dublin, Irish striker Patrick Moore experienced a bittersweet situation. During a World Cup qualifier, Moore scored four goals against Belgium, but his team didn't win: they drew 4-4. Two of the visitors' goals came from François Vanden Eynde, who became the first substitute to score – in this case, twice – in a World Cup match. Moore registered another goal in the qualifier against the Netherlands on 8 April 1934 at the Olympic Stadium in Amsterdam. However, Ireland lost 5-2 and missed out on the World Cup.

* Incredibly, Italy had to participate in the qualifying round to compete in their home World Cup. On

ITALY 1934

25 March, two months before the start of the competition, the *Azzurri* defeated Greece 4-0 in Milan. The rematch, agreed upon in Athens, was never played: the Greek team chose to withdraw rather than suffer another frustration. Almost 60 years later, a journalistic investigation revealed that Italian officials had paid a large sum of money to their Greek counterparts in exchange for their resignation and the cancellation of the second match.

* Another unusual case involved Mexico and the United States. As the representatives of the two teams could not agree on the venue for the match they would play to determine who would secure the only spot reserved for the Caribbean, Central, and North American countries, both teams accepted a proposal from the World Cup organisers: travel to Italy and face each other at the National Fascist Party Stadium in Rome. On 24 May, three days before the start of the World Cup itself, the United States defeated their continental rivals 4-2. Aldo 'Buff' Donelli, a forward born in Pennsylvania and son of Neapolitan parents, scored all four goals.

* Argentina's representation was made up of amateur players. Because most clubs had left the official association to form the first professional league, the entity had to assemble a team with players from seven affiliated squads and some inexperienced players from different provinces. The Argentine delegation crossed the Atlantic Ocean and the Mediterranean Sea aboard a ship that took two weeks to dock in Italy, and they were immediately eliminated after losing 3-2 to Sweden in Bologna.

* As had happened at the Olympic Games, Egypt once again became the first team from their continent to participate in a World Cup. The North Africans lost 4-2 to Hungary on their debut. Both Egyptian goals were scored by Abdelrahman Fawzi, a record for Egypt in World Cups shared with Mohamed Salah, who scored both of his goals in two matches in Russia in 2018.

* The first-round matches were played on the same day, 27 May, in Rome, Milan, Naples, Turin, Trieste, Bologna, Florence and Genoa. It was particularly striking that all the countries that had participated in Uruguay four years earlier and travelled to Italy for the second tournament lost in the first round: Belgium, 5-2 to Germany; France, 3-2 to Austria; Romania, 2-1 to Czechoslovakia; the United States, 7-1 to the hosts; Argentina, 3-2 to Sweden; and Brazil, 3-1 to Spain.

* The official ball was called the Federale 102. It was manufactured by a local company called Ente Centrale Approvvigionamento Sportivi, based in Rome. The covering consisted of 13 brown leather panels held together with a cotton cord. This string was softer than the leather strap used in 1930, and did not cause injuries to the players when headed.

* The Italian squad included four Argentine-born players in Enrique Guaita, Raimundo Orsi, Attilio José Demaría and Luis Monti; the latter two having represented Argentina in Uruguay four years earlier. Italy also had one Brazilian, Amphilóquio Guarisi Marques, registered as Anfilogino Guarisi, the surname of his Italian mother.

ITALY 1934

* The 90-minute last-16 match between France and Austria in Turin ended 1-1. Therefore, Dutch referee Johannes van Moorsel implemented a regulation that had never been used before in the World Cup: extra time. In the added period, consisting of two 15-minute halves, goals by Anton Schall and Josef Bican cemented Austria's victory.

* The Spain staff included a chef named Francisco Blanch, who prepared Basque and Catalan dishes for the players. Until that moment, no national federation had ever considered having a cook as part of their setup. Furthermore, Basque midfielder Pedro Regueiro was unable to play in Italy, even though he was one of Real Madrid's biggest stars at the time. A few days before the start of the tournament, Spanish coach Amadeo García explained that Regueiro did 'not have his father's permission' to travel to Italy because he also soon had 'final exams that will affect his future'. In addition to being a footballer, Regueiro was a university student.

* Switzerland featured a forward named Leopold Kielholz, who did not seem like a formidable player: he was only 5ft 7in (1.71 metres) tall and played with thick glasses due to a severe myopia. However, on the pitch, Kielholz was an indomitable striker: he scored twice against the Netherlands in the first round and another against Czechoslovakia in the quarter-finals. Switzerland ultimately fell 3-2 to the Czechs, but the small, bespectacled Kielholz managed an enviable record of 1.5 goals per game played in Italy.

* During the quarter-final between Austria and Hungary on 31 May at the Stadio del Littoriale in Bologna, an incident occurred that has to date never

been repeated in the World Cup: a player, Hungary's István Avar, missed two penalties. The first came in the opening half, with Austria leading 1-0. The second was after half-time, with the Austrians now 2-0 ahead. A short while later, Italian referee Francesco Mattea awarded a third penalty to Hungary, which this time ended up in the net, albeit by another player: György Sárosi. Austria won 2-1.

* Italy are the only team in World Cup history to have played three matches in four days. The first was the quarter-final against Spain, on 31 May in Florence. As the match ended 1-1 after 90 minutes and half an hour of extra time (the first draw in the World Cup), the two teams, as required by the regulations at the time, met again at the same venue the following day. In the rematch, the *Azzurri* won 1-0 with a goal from Giuseppe Meazza. Two days later, on 3 June, Italy travelled to Milan to defeat Austria 1-0 in the semi-final, thanks to a goal from Enrique Orsi.

* Spanish players and journalists who travelled to the World Cup reported that the Iberian team were treated unfairly by Belgian referee Louis Baert, who was in charge of their match against Italy in the quarter-finals, accusing him of having been bribed by the Italian government. Everyone agreed that, seconds before the home side's equaliser, visiting goalkeeper Ricardo Zamora suffered a violent blow from centre-forward Angelo Schiavio, resulting in two broken ribs. They also pointed out that Baert unfairly disallowed a Spanish goal for an alleged offside offence that they said hadn't occurred. Upon returning home, the Spanish players were given a heroes' welcome. They were invited to numerous

banquets and parties, and the Madrid newspaper *La Voz* awarded each of them gold medals in recognition of their 'moral victory' in the World Cup.

* 'It's impossible to win in the atmosphere they [the Italians] have prepared. We have to resign ourselves and let the Blues take the title. But this won't stop us from declaring that their football isn't the best, and that they won't win the title of world champions fairly. These are unacceptable brutalities, and if they're not corrected, they will disrupt the true sport.' Austrian coach Hugo Meisl when speaking to the press, furious about his team's defeat to Italy in the semi-final played on 3 June at the San Siro stadium in Milan.

* After Germany were eliminated in the semi-finals by Czechoslovakia, coach Otto Nerz warned that, due to numerous injuries and the withdrawal of midfielder Rudolf Gramlich, from the 18 players he had taken to the World Cup, he had only ten left to face Austria in the third-place match on 7 June in Naples. Urged to complete his squad, Nerz sent a telegram calling up Alemannia Aachen defender and star player Reinhold Münzenberg. After receiving the urgent message, Münzenberg called the hotel where the delegation was staying and explained to Nerz's assistant coach, Sepp Herberger, that he couldn't travel: he and his fiancée had planned to get married on the day of the play-off. Herberger replied, 'A wedding can be postponed, but a World Cup can't.' Moved, Münzenberg convinced his future wife to postpone the ceremony and travelled to Naples. Thanks to Münzenberg's great work, Germany defeated Austria 3-2 and won the bronze medal.

* The first World Cup third-place play-off – Yugoslavia had refused to play against the United States in 1930 – had an added twist: upon entering the field at the Giorgio Ascarelli Stadium in Naples, both teams were dressed in their traditional uniforms of white shirts, black shorts, and black socks. Italian referee Albino Carraro summoned captains Fritz Szepan (Germany) and Josef Smistik (Austria) and drew lots, which determined that the Austrians would exchange their jerseys for the light-blue ones of Napoli. Thus, for the first time in the World Cup, a national team wore the shirt of a club side.

* Numerous journalistic sources claim that, before the start of the World Cup, fascist dictator Benito Mussolini threatened the Italian coach, Vittorio Pozzo, and the players with severe punishments if they did not win the tournament. Years later, one of the players, Luis Monti, revealed that the night before the final between Italy and Czechoslovakia, Mussolini had dinner with the referee designated for the momentous match, the Swede Ivan Eklind, who had also officiated in the home team's victory over Austria. On 10 June 1934, at the National Fascist Party Stadium in Rome, Italy won 2-1 and were crowned world champions.

* The Italian victory was not easy. After the first half of the final ended goalless, the Czechs took the lead in the 71st minute with a goal from Antonín Puč. Italy equalised ten minutes later, thanks to Raimundo Orsi. The 90 minutes ended in a draw, and for the first time, a World Cup Final had to go into extra time: just five minutes into the added

period, Angelo Schiavio scored the goal that gave the home team the title.

* Vittorio Pozzo was also a journalist for the Turin newspaper *La Stampa*. He even used to write commentaries for his own team's matches. After the victory against Czechoslovakia, Pozzo wrote an article in which he remarked, 'There is nothing in the world that surpasses the satisfaction of a duty performed conscientiously, truthfully, tenaciously, studiously, prudently. It is a satisfaction that compensates for everything.' He also remarked that 'the World Cup could not have had a more worthy epilogue' than Italy's triumph, in 'a kind of apotheosis of football', with 'varied tactics, techniques, and quick flashes that also shone with beauty'.

* The 1934 World Cup remains equal with Uruguay 1930 as the tournament with the fewest goals, although its average was higher than that of the South American tournament: 4.12 goals per game. Eighteen matches were played in Uruguay, one more than in Italy.

* Oldřich Nejedlý died without being recognised as the top scorer in Italy, at least not alone. When Nejedlý died on 11 June 1990, official statistics indicated that three players had scored the most goals: the Czech striker, Germany's Edmund Conen, and Italy's Angelo Schiavio, all with four. Nejedlý was credited with one goal against Romania in the first round, another against Switzerland in the quarter-final, and two against Germany in the semi-final, which the runners-up won 3-1. However, in November 2006, an investigation led by the striker's descendants determined that Czechoslovakia's second goal

against Germany was not the work of midfielder Rudolf Krčil, but rather Nejedlý. The absence of numbers on the jerseys and the timing of the goal – several players charged together toward the German penalty area after Antonín Puč's shot from the edge of the box bounced off the crossbar – confused Italian referee Rinaldo Barlassina and journalists in the press box, who believed the ball had been kicked into the net by Krčil. Sixteen years after his death, Nejedlý was declared the sole top scorer of the 1934 World Cup, with five goals.

Statistical focus – teams with the most World Cup matches:

Country	Matches	Appearances
Brazil	114	22
Germany	112	20
Argentina	88	18
Italy	83	18
England	74	16

France 1938

* France's selection as the host country for the 1938 World Cup was finalised during the 1936 Olympic Games held in Berlin. Meeting at the Kroll Opera House in the German capital, the FIFA committee resolved that the third edition would be held in Europe and not in the Americas, as had been verbally agreed upon in 1929 when Uruguay had been chosen to host the first event. The votes of the delegates, mostly from the Old World, leaned toward France over Argentina, the only candidate from its region. Among other reasons, the committee members argued that they wanted to pay tribute to Jules Rimet, FIFA president and 'father' of the tournament, but the truth was that none of the European teams wanted to repeat the odyssey of crossing the Atlantic Ocean on a ship. Offended, the Argentine delegates withdrew from the tournament and tried to convince the rest of the American nations not to participate. Associations from countries such as Uruguay, the United States, Mexico, El Salvador, Colombia, Costa Rica, and Suriname withdrew their registrations and joined the protest, but the World Cup featured two American teams that did agree to play: Brazil and Cuba. Both teams qualified without having to participate in a qualifying round.

* For the first time, the defending champions and the host country were given automatic entry without

having to play in the qualifying round. In addition to Italy, France, Brazil, and Cuba, two other teams reached the World Cup without having to play in the qualifying round: Romania, after Egypt's resignation, and the Dutch East Indies (now Indonesia), due to the withdrawal of their only rivals in the vast Asian region, Japan.

* For this championship, the organisers decided to repeat the system of 1934: 16 participants divided into a direct elimination competition. If a match ended level after 90 minutes and half an hour of extra time, the two teams would have to meet again a few days later, except for the final: the tournament regulations stipulated that if neither contender led after 120 minutes, both would be declared 'champions by equal merit'.

* Austria qualified after defeating Latvia on 5 October 1937. However, on 12 March 1938, Nazi dictator Adolf Hitler ordered the invasion of the neighbouring nation and annexed it to Germany. A month later, through a direct vote, 99.7 per cent of the Austrian population agreed to their country becoming a German province. Faced with this political conflict, which effectively nullified Austria's status as an independent country, the World Cup organisers offered the vacant spot to England, but the Football Association rejected the invitation. As a result, Sweden, who had been drawn as Austria's opponent in the last 16, advanced to the quarter-finals without playing.

* Several of the Austrian players, who had been left without a country to represent, agreed to join Germany. Josef Stroh, Rudolf Raftl (who had

already been part of Austria's squad in 1934 without playing), Wilhelm Hahnemann, Leopold Neumer, Johann Pesser, Willibald Schmaus and Stefan Skoumal all switched. Despite reinforcements from the *Wunderteam* (German for 'wonder team', as the Austrian side was known in the 1930s), Germany were eliminated in the first round, falling to Switzerland after two matches that ended 1-1 and 4-2.

* It wasn't only Austria experiencing serious political problems during those years: Spain had been immersed in a terrible civil war since July 1936. Despite this, two delegates from the Iberian country travelled to Paris to witness the World Cup and participate in a FIFA Congress, one from each side in the conflict: Francoists and Republicans.

* The Spanish Civil War also affected the qualifying match between Switzerland and Portugal: as the Swiss refused to cross Spain to face the Portuguese in Lisbon, the delegates from both teams agreed that the tie would be decided in a single match on a neutral ground, the Civic Arena in Milan. There, Switzerland won 2-1 thanks to a rare bit of good fortune: the Portuguese hit goalkeeper Willy Huber's posts three times, and striker João Cruz, who had not missed from the penalty spot in three years, fired a spot kick into the stands.

* For the 1938 World Cup, each participating team was required to submit two photographs and a résumé of each player, at the request of FIFA observers. The official ball, an Allen brand, was made by a Parisian company.

* The performance of the Dutch East Indies team is, without a doubt, one of the worst in World Cup

history. In their only match – in fact, they are yet to again participate in the finals, not even as Indonesia – played on 5 June at the Vélodrome Municipal in Reims, they lost 6-0 to Hungary. Considering the averages between matches played and goals scored, the Dutch East Indies have a figure of -6 goals per match, the lowest of all the teams to have participated in the 22 World Cups.

* Switzerland's victory over Germany in the first round, following a 1-1 draw on 4 June at the Parc des Princes in Paris and then the rematch five days later at the same venue, had a huge impact. In the decisive match, the Germans took a 2-0 lead. Switzerland pulled one back in the 42nd minute but were soon down to ten men: forward Georges Aeby suffered a severe blow to the head and had to be stretchered off the field, unconscious. Thirteen minutes into the second half, due to regulations prohibiting substitutions, Aeby returned to the field with his head fully bandaged. Despite the knock, he managed to provide an assist for Fredy Bickel and two for André Abegglen to turn the score around and cement Switzerland's 4-2 victory. The violent contusion prevented Aeby from playing three days later, in Lille against Hungary; in his absence, the Hungarians won 2-0.

* György Sárosi, one of the best Hungarian footballers of his time, was working as a lawyer for a prestigious firm in Budapest. A few days before the start of the World Cup, having found himself tied up with some very important cases, Sárosi withdrew from his country's squad. However, at the insistence of his team-mates and club coach Alfréd Schaffer, the

striker, who was also the side's captain, reconsidered his decision and travelled to France. Sárosi not only established himself as the best Hungarian player, but also the team's top scorer: he scored two goals against the East Indies, one against Switzerland, one against Sweden, and one against Italy in the final. Upon returning to Hungary, he resigned as a lawyer. Sárosi played until 1948 and then continued a prolific career as a coach for clubs such as Ferencváros, Juventus, and AS Roma.

* An investigation based on newspaper reports determined that, during the 3-3 draw between Cuba and Romania in Toulouse on 5 June in the first round, Caribbean native José Magriñá scored the first 'Olympic goal' in World Cup history, beating goalkeeper Dumitru Pavlovici with a direct shot from a corner.

* The replay between Cuba and Romania had a very curious twist: Cuba coach José Tapia decided that, on 9 June, the same 11 players who had played in the first game would take the field at the Chapou Stadium in Toulouse. But one of them, goalkeeper Benito Carvajales, asked Tapia to let his substitute, Juan Ayra, take his place because he had been invited to participate in the match broadcast by a Cuban radio station and preferred to be a commentator rather than a player. With Ayra in goal, Cuba won 2-1. For the next match, against Sweden at the Fort Carreé Stadium in Antibes, Tapia returned to the starting line-up because that game would not be broadcast on the radio. The 'commentator' conceded eight goals and Cuba were eliminated.

* The last-16 match between Brazil and Poland began with a peculiarity: the two teams' key stars – Leônidas and Ernest Wilimowski, respectively – arrived at the World Cup in poor health. Leônidas was suffering from a troublesome ear infection, while Wilimowski was in pain from a severe toothache, but the offending tooth was not extracted because it would have required several days of rest. On 5 June in Strasbourg, Leônidas and Wilimowski played one of the most spectacular clashes in World Cup history: the Brazilian scored three times; the Pole four. The South Americans won 6-5, and poor Wilimowski, the first player to score four in a World Cup match, left France after being eliminated in the first round but with a curious and remarkable record having averaged four goals per appearance.

* The day before the quarter-final between France and Italy, scheduled for 12 June at the Stade Olympique de Colombes in Paris, Belgian referee Louis Baert called the captains, Étienne Mattler and Giuseppe Meazza, to conduct the draw to decide which team would retain their blue shirts and which would wear an alternative colour. The coin toss favoured the home team, so the Italian kit men prepared two alternatives: one white, the colour that the team would normally wear in these circumstances, and another black, which they had never worn before. To decide which shirts to use, the senior players consulted dictator Benito Mussolini, who ordered his men to take the field wearing black shirts, the representative colour of fascism. Italy defeated France 3-1, and for the first time in the history of the World Cup, the host country did not play in the final.

FRANCE 1938

* The 1-1 draw between Brazil and Czechoslovakia at the Parc Lescure in Bordeaux on 12 June in the quarter-finals resembled more a martial arts exhibition than a football match. Hungarian referee Pál von Hertzka sent off Brazil's Zezé Procópio for kicking two opponents, and his team-mate Arthur Machado and the Czechs' Jan Říha – for punching each other. Despite the double punishment, Brazil finished the game with an extra player, as two Czechs were forced off due to serious injuries: forward Oldřich Nejedlý, who scored his team's penalty, suffered a fractured bone in his right foot, and midfielder Josef Košťálek received a blow to the liver that prevented him from continuing. Shortly before the 90-minute mark, with the score tied at 1-1, goalkeeper František Plánička was kicked, fracturing the radius of his right arm. However, the courageous player remained in his position until the 30 minutes of extra time was completed, during which the score remained unchanged. The rematch two days later, with the injured and dismissed players missing, was won 2-1 by Brazil.

* 'If we lose, I'll walk back to Budapest,' read a remarkable comment by Hungary's coach, Károly Dietz, to the press the day before the semi-final against Sweden, which the Scandinavians went into after crushing Cuba 8-0. Hungary won 5-1, and Dietz was spared a 1,500km stroll.

* Brazil's coach, Adhemar Pimenta, made one of the biggest mistakes in World Cup – and football – history: to face Italy in the semi-final on 16 June at the Vélodrome in Marseille, he decided to rest his best player, the ferocious striker Leônidas, who

had scored no fewer than five goals in the three matches over the two first rounds: three against Poland, two against Czechoslovakia. Without their star man, Brazil lost 2-1 to Italy and were relegated to playing only for third place, against Sweden.

* 'Leônidas is too tired. I'm saving him for next Sunday, when we'll play the final in Paris. I have absolute faith in our victory,' said a boastful Pimenta ahead of the semi-final.

* In the third-place match, on 19 June at the Parc Lescure in Bordeaux, Brazil defeated Sweden 4-2, with two goals from Leônidas, who became the 1938 tournament's top scorer with seven goals – despite Pimenta leaving him out for the semi-final.

* On the day of the final, on 19 June at the Stade Olympique de Colombes, French president Albert Lebrun was present. Lebrun, poorly informed, asked Jules Rimet, sitting next to him, 'Where are the French?' Rimet, blushing at the absence of the Gallic team on the field, pointed his index finger at referee George Capdeville. 'There you have him,' he said, 'the referee is French.'

* Several journalists who worked at the tournament agreed that Benito Mussolini's arm reached all the way to Paris. The reporters revealed that, hours before the final between Italy and Hungary, the president sent a telegram to the Parisian hotel where the *Azzurri* were staying. The message, addressed to the 22 players and coach Vittorio Pozzo, was very brief, *'Vincere o morire.'* It translates as win or die. Italy won 4-2, and no one died.

FRANCE 1938

* This was the first time that a host country had not been crowned champions. Italy also became the first country to win two consecutive World Cups. Brazil would match that record in 1958 in Sweden and 1962 in Chile.

Statistical focus – teams with the most World Cup wins:

Country	Wins	Appearances
Brazil	76	22
Germany	68	20
Argentina	47	18
Italy	45	18
France	39	16

BRAZIL 1950

* After two editions of the World Cup were suspended due to the progress and consequences of the Second World War – which began in September 1939 and ended six years later, in September 1945 – a FIFA Congress held in Luxembourg in July 1946 awarded Brazil the honour of hosting the fourth World Cup. Thus, the competition returned to the Americas 20 years after its debut in Uruguay. FIFA banned entries from West Germany and Japan, countries that had been on the defeated side in the war, but did allow Italy, one of their allies, to participate. Why? Because the *Azzurri* were the reigning champions, and the president of the Italian federation, Ottorino Barassi, had guarded the trophy throughout the conflict. Barassi kept the golden sculpture hidden in his house – inside a shoebox!

* During the FIFA Congress meetings held in Luxembourg, the 46 participating delegates approved the trophy being renamed as the Jules Rimet Trophy in honour of the FIFA president, who had just completed 25 consecutive years in the distinguished position.

* For the first time, British teams – England, Scotland, Wales, and the current Northern Ireland team – agreed to compete for a place at the World Cup, using the British Home Championship, a tournament in which all four nations had participated since 1883, as

a UK-only qualifying round. Due to the low number of entries, FIFA offered places to the top two teams. England won the championship and travelled to Brazil, but Scotland, the runners-up, chose not to participate.

* The rest of the qualifying rounds proved rather chaotic. In Group B, Turkey defeated Syria 7-0, but their next opponents, Austria, opted to withdraw without playing. Turkey also decided not to travel to Brazil. Switzerland defeated Luxembourg and qualified thanks to Belgium, the other contenders, refusing to participate in the tournament anyway. In South America, Argentina, Colombia, Ecuador, and Peru decided not to compete, allowing Uruguay, Paraguay, Chile, and Bolivia to secure their tickets to Brazil without breaking a sweat.

* At the 1948 London Olympics, India narrowly lost 2-1 to France, but the result could have been different as they missed a penalty when the score was 1-1. In that game, most of the Indian squad members played barefoot, as was the custom on the fields of Bombay and New Delhi. This should not have been accepted by Swedish referee Gunnar Dahlner, as it was a violation of the regulations regarding players' attire, given the danger posed to bare feet. A few months before the World Cup in Brazil, due to the low participation rate and the withdrawal of Burma, the Philippines and Indonesia, FIFA decided to invite India, but clarified that they would not be allowed to play barefoot. The players, offended, chose to decline the invite.

* For the development of this tournament, FIFA determined that the first phase would comprise

four groups of four teams each. However, due to withdrawals – several of them at the last minute, after the first phase had already been drawn – only 12 nations travelled to compete alongside Brazil, the hosts. Thus, the initial round was severely unbalanced, with two groups of four teams, one of three, and one of two – Uruguay and Bolivia.

* For the second round, the organisers devised an unusual scheme: the winners of each initial group advanced to a final round-robin quadrangular tournament, where they faced each other. Brazil 1950 was the only World Cup in history that did not have a conventional final. Brazil and Uruguay went into the last match of the quadrangular with a chance of winning, so the game between them was, in essence, a final. However, based on previous results, a draw was enough for Brazil to be crowned champions. This schedule could have led to a very different outcome, as one of the other teams could have won the World Cup without having to play in the final match of the tournament. FIFA took note and this ridiculous system was never used again.

* After Brazil was confirmed as the host nation, the Rio de Janeiro state government ordered the building of a gigantic stadium, known worldwide as the Maracanã. Its construction took almost two years, involving 11,000 workers, half a million bags of cement, and ten million kilograms of iron. In 1964, the stadium was officially named Jornalista Mário Filho, but it is popularly known as the Maracanã for the name of a narrow stream that runs very close by. During the 1950 World Cup, the monumental stadium hosted eight of the 22 matches, including

the opener on 24 June, when Brazil crushed Mexico 4-0 in front of 82,000 spectators, and the crucial game, played on 16 July between Brazil and Uruguay. Officially, 175,000 tickets were sold that day, but various newspaper reports claim that the number of spectators rose to 200,000, due to the large number of special guests and those who managed to enter without a ticket.

* Numbers on the backs of players' jerseys became mandatory for Brazil 1950. Switzerland's Fredy Bickel and Sweden's Erik Nilsson, who had played in the 1938 World Cup in France, were the only men to participate in the tournament before and after the Second World War. The official match ball, the Superball Duplo T, was made from wedges of light-brown leather.

* All the teams competing used aeroplanes as a means of transport, except for Italy. The defending champions preferred to cross the Atlantic Ocean by boat. This unusual choice was due to the fact that, among Italians, the memory of the *Superga* tragedy was still fresh: on 4 May 1949, a plane carrying the players and coaching staff of Torino, who were returning from playing in Portugal, crashed shortly before arriving in the Piedmontese capital into a basilica in the town of Superga. The sea transfer complicated the team's preparation: in the first training session, all the balls ended up in the ocean. Upon arriving several days later in Santos, a port town in São Paulo, the Italian players were poorly trained and slightly overweight. In their first match, on 25 June at the Estádio do Pacaembu, the *Azzurri* were defeated 3-2 by Sweden; they were eliminated

four days later when the Swedes drew with Paraguay. Italy thus became the first holders to fail to advance past the first round of the following competition.

* 'I can only be blamed for one mistake: not insisting on flying the players to Brazil.' An unusual excuse from Italian coach Ferruccio Novo, after his team's elimination.

* England made their World Cup debut with a 2-0 victory over Chile on 25 June at the Maracanã. For their second game, four days later in Belo Horizonte against the supposedly weak United States – who had been beaten 3-1 by Spain in their opener – coach Walter Winterbottom preferred to field several of his substitute players and save his stars for the group-deciding match against the Spaniards. London bookmakers were offering a US triumph at odds of 500/1; the English had a terrible afternoon, and the Americans pulled off an unexpected 1-0 victory. The scorer of the only goal, Joe Gaetjens, was Haitian and had not become a US citizen. The sports editor of the *New York Times* received a telex announcing the team's victory, read it, crumpled the paper, and threw it in a trash can: he thought it was a joke!

* 'Never before has an English team played so badly.' A categorical statement from *The Times* after the Three Lions' defeat against the United States.

* Three days after beating Mexico in the first match, Brazil – then wearing an all-white kit – travelled to the Estádio do Pacaembu in São Paulo, where they drew 2-2 with Switzerland. After the game, the home team's coach, Flávio Costa, was surrounded by hundreds of furious Brazilian fans who attempted to attack him as he tried to board

the squad bus. Several police officers struggled with the supporters and managed to prevent the attack. In addition to the disappointing draw, Costa was unpopular in São Paulo because he had spent most of his career to that point playing or coaching in Rio de Janeiro.

* On 1 July, Brazil played their third match, against Yugoslavia at the Maracanã. Their victory was secured by an unusual event: the Europeans started the match with ten men! As they walked on to the pitch, Željko Čajkovski slipped and injured his head on the iron frame of one of the sliding doors of the tunnel. The impact left Čajkovski with a deep cut on his forehead, forcing him to return to the dressing room for medical attention. After receiving four stitches, the striker, with his head bandaged, came on to the pitch to complete his team, the Yugoslavs already losing 1-0 to a goal by Ademir in the fourth minute. Welsh referee Benjamin Griffiths had ordered the match to start despite Yugoslavia having only ten men. They never recovered, and in the second half Brazil scored their second goal in a 2-0 victory.

* On 2 July, when Mexico and Switzerland appeared on the pitch of the Estádio dos Eucaliptos – then the home of the Internacional club of Porto Alegre – Swedish referee Ivan Eklind decided that the Aztecs' burgundy jerseys were too similar in tone to the Swiss's deep red. Eklind called the captains, Horacio Casarín and Roger Bocquet, and tossed a coin to determine which of the two teams would remove their uniforms and put on the blue shirts provided by a representative of the local club, Esporte

Clube Cruzeiro, who had just played in a preliminary friendly. Casarín won the toss, but decided to offer Switzerland the choice of whether or not to keep their official jerseys. Noticing that the loaned shirts were soaked with sweat, Bocquet opted to keep the red ones. The Mexicans then put on the borrowed, dirty shirts, insulting the gentleman Casarín. Switzerland won 2-1, and Casarín at least earned a consolation prize: the captain scored his team's goal in the 89th minute.

* In the final round-robin tournament, Brazil thrashed Sweden 7-1, with a four-goal effort from Ademir, and Spain 6-1, while Uruguay drew 2-2 with Spain and narrowly defeated Sweden 3-2. In the final game, on 16 July at the Maracanā, a draw would have been enough for Brazil to win the World Cup for the first time. On the morning of the match, Brazilian newspaper *Gazeta do Povo* published a picture of the squad accompanied by the unusual phrase, 'A few more hours and we'll be world champions.' Minutes before kick-off, a Uruguayan official gathered the players and told them, 'Guys, don't worry too much. Just try not to concede six goals. With four we are okay.' However, before taking the field, with the stands packed with 200,000 home fans, captain Obdulio Varela congregated his team-mates inside the tunnel and shouted, 'Don't look to the crowd, those on the outside are made of wood. And "fulfil" ... only if we are champions!'

* The referee for the match between Brazil and Uruguay, Englishman George Reader, was 53 years and 236 days old. He is the oldest referee to officiate a match in the history of the World Cup.

* The first half of the decisive game ended scoreless. Two minutes into the second half, Albino Friaça Cardoso made it 1-0 for Brazil. Uruguay needed two goals to win the World Cup, and they got them with a shot from Juan Schiaffino in the 66th minute and another from Alcides Ghiggia in the 79th. The home team tried to equalise, but couldn't beat goalkeeper Roque Máspoli. Uruguay won 2-1 and achieved one of the greatest feats in the history of the World Cup; their triumph will for ever be recorded as *El Maracanazo* ('The Maracanã Smash').

* 'It was the first time in my life I heard something other than noise. I felt the silence,' said Uruguayan midfielder Juan Schiaffino, scorer of the first goal of *El Maracanazo*.

* The Brazilian players managed to leave the Maracanã thanks to a massive police operation: hundreds of angry fans tried to attack the defeated squad. Coach Flávio Costa remained locked in the dressing room for two days, fearing he would be lynched as soon as he set foot outside the stadium. He only agreed to leave his hiding place when a relative handed him a set of clothes with which to disguise himself. Almost 48 hours after the final whistle, Costa left the Maracanã – dressed as a woman!

* 'The highest sentence in my country for committing a crime is 30 years. I've been serving 50 years for a crime I didn't commit.' The lament of Brazilian goalkeeper Moacir Barbosa a few days before his death in April 2000. Because of the two goals conceded against Uruguay, Barbosa went from being a great star to becoming the most hated man in Brazil.

* When the champions returned to Montevideo, the Uruguayan Football Association ordered gold and silver medals to be minted to reward the heroes. The silver ones went to the players, and the gold ones to the officials who had accompanied the squad, including the one who had urged the players not to lose by six goals. The gesture infuriated the players. 'If we had known, we would have lost on purpose,' asserted Obdulio Varela.

* *El Maracanazo* also put an end to the all-white kit that Brazil had used since 1919. Convinced that this attire brought bad luck, in 1953 the Brazilian Sports Confederation organised a design competition to choose a new official kit. Participants had to combine the colours of the Brazilian flag: yellow, green, blue, and white. The organisation received some 300 designs and declared 19-year-old Aldyr García Schlee as the winner; he presented a yellow shirt with the collar and sleeve cuffs in green, blue shorts, and white socks, a combination that is now recognised as one of the most famous in world football.

Statistical focus – teams with the most World Cup match losses:

Country	Losses	Tournaments
Mexico	28	17
Argentina	24	18
Germany	23	20
Serbia†	22	13
Uruguay	21	14

† According to FIFA statistics, this includes tournament appearances by Yugoslavia, Serbia and Montenegro, and Serbia.

Switzerland 1954

* Switzerland was elected as the host of the 1954 World Cup on the same day as Brazil, at the FIFA Congress held in Luxembourg in July 1946. The Swiss bid was crowned unchallenged. While most European states were focused on recovering from the devastation caused by the Second World War, the Alpine nation, which had remained neutral during the conflict, had the necessary financial backing to host the tournament.

* The qualifiers offered two debuts: for the first time, teams from South America and Asia competed for a place in football's most important tournament. After Argentina and Peru withdrew, Brazil prevailed in a triangular tournament against Paraguay and Chile. On the other side of the planet, South Korea and Japan played a two-legged qualifier in the same venue, the Meiji Jingu Gaien Stadium in Tokyo. The Koreans qualified after a 5-1 victory and a 2-2 draw.

* In Europe, the division of Germany after the Second World War led to the formation of three states: the Federal Republic of Germany (FRG), in charge of the western portion of the former nation; the German Democratic Republic (GDR), which controlled the eastern part of the country and maintained close political ties with the Soviet Union; and the Saarland, a small region in the south-west where the United Nations had created a protectorate supervised by

France. The three 'nations' were accepted by FIFA, and in the qualifying round, chance would have it that the FRG and Saarland shared a group with Norway. West Germany easily won after three wins and a draw from their four matches.

* For the second time, the British Home Championship served as a qualifying round for England, Scotland, Wales, and Northern Ireland. The tournament was won by England, but in this case, the Scots, who finished second, agreed to compete in Switzerland.

* After the Soviet Union withdrew due to political issues, Group 6 of the European qualifiers became a head-to-head clash between Spain and Turkey, which suggested easy qualification for the Spaniards. This was even more so after they won the first leg 4-1 in Madrid. In Istanbul, the second leg was marred by the home team's rough play and the carelessness of German referee Emil Schmetzer: the Turks won 1-0, and because goal difference was not taken into account at the time, the two teams had to face each other in a play-off at Rome's Stadio Olimpico. There, after a 2-2 draw in 90 minutes and half an hour of added time with no further goals, the match was decided by a draw: a boy named Franco Gemma, son of an employee at the Roman stadium, put his hand into a cup containing two pieces of paper with the team names and picked out the one that said Turkey, thus securing their first World Cup qualification.

* The draw for the groups in the first round in Switzerland may well be considered the most unusual in the history of football. Why? The procedure was held in Zurich on 31 November 1953, before the qualifying rounds had even ended. The delegates who

SWITZERLAND 1954

chose the seeded teams ignored the home team, a feat that would never be repeated, and West Germany, the eventual champions. But that point would be trivial compared to other truly serious decisions: the committee named defending champions Uruguay, France and Austria (who had qualified a few days before that meeting), Brazil (who had yet to face Paraguay and Chile), Hungary (who advanced without competing due to the withdrawal of Poland and the Netherlands), Italy (who, despite having beaten Egypt 2-1 in Cairo, still had their second leg in Milan to play), and England, who had not completed the British Home Championship and had a key game against Scotland pending. But the most striking thing of all is that the committee named Spain as the eighth seed – four months before they lost their qualifying round to Turkey! Although it may seem incredible, for the only time in the history of the World Cup, a privileged place in the initial phase of the tournament was assigned to a country that had never qualified.

* The designation of the seeded teams wasn't the only blunder by the tournament organisers. For this fifth World Cup, FIFA abandoned the system used in Brazil 1950, with a final group stage to determine the champions. However, its directors nevertheless managed to complicate matters considerably: for the first round, they assembled four groups of four teams. Instead of having teams play against each other, the two seeds were to play against the other two teams in the group, but not against each other. Apparently, the organisers' idea was to have the supposedly strongest countries meet only after the quarter-finals. The unusual idea was misguided because, contrary to the

predictions of the supposed experts, play-off matches had to be added in two of the four groups. As a result, Switzerland defeated Italy twice, and Germany beat Turkey twice.

* The 1954 World Cup was the first to have matches broadcast live on television. A company based in eight European countries agreed with FIFA to broadcast nine matches, including the opening game and the final. This initiative began a relationship that would become more intense with each new edition.

* The official ball for this tournament was called the Swiss World Champion. Made by the Basel-based company Kost Sport, the ball was covered with 18 panels of yellow-dyed leather, 'a colour more visible to the human eye' according to its designers.

* Ahead of the tournament, FIFA issued a series of mandatory guidelines for referees. Some seemed logical, such as prohibiting drinking alcohol on days when they were required to act as referees or linesmen, or advising them to go to bed early the night before a match. But others were striking, such as 'taking a cold shower in the morning, straight after getting up, and another before going to bed' or 'doing a jump rope exercise for 15 minutes every day'. However, the most disastrous was that 'in the event of the referee's death during a match, the game will be immediately terminated'. A provision that, fortunately, no referee had to implement.

* In Group 2, South Korea produced one of the worst performances in the history of the World Cup: they played two matches, conceded 16 goals, and scored none. On 17 June at the Hardturm-Stadion in Zurich, the Asian squad suffered a humiliating 9-0

SWITZERLAND 1954

thrashing by Hungary. Three days later, at the Stade des Charmilles in Geneva, they were again hit by a barrage of goals from Turkey: 7-0. The average age of the Korean players was 31, one of the highest in the competition's history.

* Scotland also put in a dismal performance, losing 1-0 to Austria in Zurich on 16 June and 7-0 to Uruguay at the St. Jakob Stadium in Basel three days later. Upon returning home, the Scottish players blamed their defeats on their football association's officials: believing the climate in mountainous Switzerland would be cold, the officials bought sets of long-sleeved shirts made of very thick wool. The warm tops proved a nightmare as that Swiss summer was particularly hot: most of the matches were played in temperatures between 30 and 40°C. Sunburned, the Scots were dehydrated by the second half of their match against Uruguay. The Uruguayans, dressed in lightweight, low-cut, short-sleeved shirts, scored five goals.

* 'The Scottish FA assumed Switzerland was cold because it had mountains. You'd have thought we were going on an expedition to the Antarctic,' said Scottish defender Tommy Docherty, trying to find an explanation for the humiliating defeat to Uruguay.

* Hungary arrived in Switzerland as the leading contenders to win the World Cup. Olympic champions at the 1952 Helsinki Games, the Hungarians appeared with a 31-match unbeaten run of 27 wins and four draws. Two of those victories had come against England, in friendlies: on 25 November 1953, they humiliated England 6-3 at Wembley, and on 23 May 1954 they repeated the

thrashing, 7-1 in Budapest. Hungary were captained by the extraordinary Ferenc Puskás, who had actually changed his original surname, Purczeld, to Puskás, which in Hungarian means 'rifleman'. In Switzerland, Hungary started their campaign with a flurry of goals: in their first two group stage matches they humiliated South Korea 9-0 in Zurich and West Germany 8-3 in Basel (with four goals from Sándor Kocsis, equalling a record previously held only by Poland's Ernest Wilimowski and Brazil's Ademir).

* Italy and Switzerland met twice in Group 4. During the first game, in Lausanne on 17 June, *Azzurri* forward Benito Lorenzi violently kicked home defender Roger Bocquet. Brazilian referee Mário Viana verbally indicated that Lorenzi had been sent off, as red and yellow cards hadn't yet been invented. However, the Italian striker didn't leave the field: he and several of his team-mates surrounded Viana and, through shoving and threats, managed to get the official to change his decision. Switzerland won 2-1, and after the end of the match, Lorenzi, unhappy with Viana's performance, kicked him in the buttocks. FIFA didn't sanction the aggressor. After Switzerland lost 2-0 to England and Italy beat Belgium 4-1 (Lorenzi scored the fourth), they met again in a play-off in Basel on 23 June. Switzerland won 4-1 and qualified for the second round; the bellicose Lorenzi was finally eliminated from the tournament.

* 'Participating in a World Cup is like winning the lottery,' said Mexican striker Tomás Balcázar, who scored in his team's 3-2 defeat to France in the first round on 19 June.

SWITZERLAND 1954

* On 26 June at the Stade de La Pontaise in Lausanne, the highest-scoring match in World Cup history took place, the quarter-final between Austria and Switzerland. The Swiss opened a commanding lead after 19 minutes, leading 3-0. Austria recovered and scored five consecutive goals before the end of the first half (and even had a chance to increase their tally, but missed a penalty). The torrent continued, and in the second half the score reached 7-5, a total of 12 goals, which has still not been equalled or surpassed at the time of publication.

* While facing Austria, Swiss player Roger Bocquet was elbowed in the head and fainted. After being taken off the field, a doctor examined him and discovered he had a brain tumour. Bocquet underwent surgery and recovered. If he hadn't suffered the blow that led to the medical examination, his doctor said that he would have died within a few months. He passed away 40 years later, in 1994, at the age of 73.

* Also in the quarter-finals, Uruguay once again demonstrated courage. On 26 June in Basel, the South Americans defeated England – who included the famous Stanley Matthews, winner of the inaugural Ballon d'Or two years later – 4-2, despite suffering numerous setbacks. In the final minute of the first half and with the score at 1-1, midfielder and legendary captain Obdulio Varela fired a shot from about 25 yards that beat goalkeeper Gil Merrick and made it 2-1. However, as a result of that effort, Varela tore a muscle and was unable to play in the second half. Because substitutions weren't allowed at the time, Uruguay had to continue with ten men against 11 English players. However, they went 3-1 up two

minutes into the second half thanks to a run by José Schiaffino. Two of the Uruguayan forwards were soon injured, Julio Abbadie and Omar Míguez, but both decided to stay on the pitch. With effectively eight against 11, England managed to pull one back in the 68th minute, but ten minutes later Javier Ambrois launched a lightning counter-attack to make the final tally 4-2. The score remained unchanged thanks to the extraordinary performance of goalkeeper Roque Máspoli.

* Hungary's 4-2 victory over Brazil at the Wankdorfstadion in Bern came amid a violent match. The furious encounter, which went down in history as the 'Battle of Bern', featured more kicks and punches than football. English referee Arthur Ellis sent off Brazil's Nilton Santos and Hungary's József Bozsik for fighting each other, and South American forward Humberto Barbosa for punching opposing defender Gyula Lóránt. After the match, Maurinho approached Zoltán Czibor, extended his right hand, and when the Hungarian forward shook it, the Brazilian launched a left-footed shot to Czibor's jaw. The attack sparked a widespread brawl involving players, substitutes and coaching staff from both teams. FIFA observers evaluated the incident and decided that no one should be suspended: according to the report, it would have been unfair because it 'would only harm Hungary for its match against Uruguay' in the semi-finals, since the Brazilians had already been eliminated. Furthermore, the federation decided not to impose a suspension on Bozsik, despite the competition's regulations stating that dismissed players must serve at least a one-match suspension.

* On 30 June in Lausanne, Hungary defeated Uruguay 4-2 in one of the semi-finals. The victory came in extra time, after the 90 minutes had finished 2-2. This result ended an extraordinary unbeaten streak: Uruguay had gone 21 matches unbeaten in international tournaments, including the Olympic Games and the World Cup. In Paris 1924 the Uruguayans won all five of their games; in Amsterdam 1928 they recorded three consecutive victories and a 1-1 draw against Argentina in the final; in the replay, Uruguay won 2-1. In their home 1930 World Cup they won all four of their matches. In Brazil 1950, they won three times and drew with Spain. In Switzerland 1954, Uruguay defeated Czechoslovakia, Scotland, and England.

* During that match, an unusual incident occurred: forward Juan Hohberg – who was born in Argentina and had become a citizen to play for Uruguay – scored two goals to make it 2-2, and after the second one he suffered a heart attack! According to the book *The World and the World Cups* by journalist Alfredo Etchandy, after Hohberg scored the equaliser, 'His team-mates fell on him in celebration, and due to the emotion, he suffered a cardiac arrest. He was resuscitated by physical therapist Carlos Abate, who gave him coramine by mouth. When extra time began, he was still out, but shortly afterward he returned to the field and played until the end of extra time.' Other reports claim that Hohberg was 'clinically dead' and that Abate revived him using mouth-to-mouth resuscitation. The truth is that, with no substitutions possible, the striker returned to the pitch and, during extra time, took a shot that hit the post. Had that effort ended up in the net,

Hohberg would have become the first dead man to score a goal.

* The final between West Germany and Hungary is remembered as the 'Miracle of Bern', because the Germans overturned a 2-0 deficit against opponents who had crushed them 8-3 in the group stage. One of the reasons for Germany's success was the boots worn by their players, designed by Adolf Dassler, founder of the Adidas company. This innovative footwear allowed players to change studs. According to reports, at half-time and with the score at 2-2, torrential rain turned the Wankdorfstadion pitch into a mud puddle. In the dressing room, German coach Sepp Herberger ordered his players to use the longer studs provided by Dassler. Bolstered by this fabulous innovation, the Germans scored their third goal after Hungarian goalkeeper Gyula Grosics slipped in the silt. Hungary's hopes sank in the mud, and West Germany lifted the World Cup for the first time.

* 'The fastest player on the team is the ball,' said Sepp Herberger.

* Hungary hold the goals record for a single World Cup, having scored 27 times in just five matches (an average of more than five per game) in 1954.

* West Germany became the first world champions to have a pair of brothers in their squad: Fritz and Ottmar Walter. Fritz Walter's intervention proved miraculous. The striker and captain had served as a soldier in the Second World War, and after being captured by the Soviet army he was sent to a prisoner-of-war camp near the Romanian city of Sighetu Marmației. Later, when it was decided to transfer all the detainees to a forced labour camp in frozen

Siberia, a miracle saved Fritz from certain death: a sentry who had recognised him from seeing him play in a friendly match between Hungary and Germany intervened and assured the camp commanders that Walter was not German, but Austrian, and requested that the prisoner be released and sent to Vienna. The officers agreed, and Fritz returned to Kaiserslautern, his hometown in Germany, where he continued his football career, interrupted by the terrible conflict.

* Switzerland 1954 is the World Cup with the highest goal average in history. In just 26 matches, 140 goals were scored, an average of 5.38 per game. This tournament also hosted the match with the most goals: Austria 7 Switzerland 5.

Statistical focus – teams with the most drawn matches in the World Cup:

Country	*Draws*	*Tournaments*
England	22	16
Germany	21	20
Italy	21	18
Brazil	19	22
Argentina	17	18
Spain	17	16

Sweden 1958

* For the second – and likely last – time in the history of the World Cup, two European nations hosted the tournament consecutively: after 1954 in Switzerland, FIFA selected Sweden for the next event. In this case, although Argentina, Mexico, and Chile had expressed their desire to host the sixth World Cup, there were no protests or calls for boycotts. Instead, the representatives of the three American countries recognised that their economic situation would not allow them to match the quality of the stadiums Sweden already had available.

* The Soviet Union participated in the World Cup for the first time, qualifying after a tight race against Poland. Both teams defeated Finland twice and won their head-to-head matches at home. Due to the tie, the Soviets and Poles had to play once again on neutral territory so, on 24 November 1957 at the Zentralstadion in Leipzig (a city then part of the socialist German Democratic Republic), the Soviets won 2-0 and secured their place among the 16 teams competing in Sweden.

* Also making their debut in the qualifiers were Argentina. After a pass to the tournament without playing in Uruguay 1930 and Italy 1934, and missing out on France 1938, Brazil 1950, and Switzerland 1954 – the latter two due to orders from president Juan Perón – they competed for one of the three

SWEDEN 1958

South American spots, defeating Bolivia and Chile to qualify.

* Sweden 1958 remains at the time of publication the only World Cup to host the four British nations: England, Scotland, Northern Ireland, and Wales. The top three won their respective European qualifying groups, but not Wales, who finished second in Group 4, behind Czechoslovakia. Meanwhile, in the combined Asia-Africa zone – with the addition of Turkey and Cyprus – Israel advanced without playing: for political reasons, the authorities from their various opponents refused to let their national teams play them. Thus, Turkey, Indonesia, and Sudan withdrew. Israel were left without opponents, but since FIFA rules stipulated that only the host nation and the defending champions could participate in the World Cup, a draw was held among the runners-up from the European groups so that the Middle Eastern team could play at least one qualifying round. Chance favoured Wales, who defeated Israel twice, both 2-0, in Tel Aviv and Cardiff.

* Mexico qualified after thrashing the United States and Canada in the first round of qualifying, and then overcoming Costa Rica after a 2-0 home victory and a 1-1 draw in San José in the final round. In the second leg, played on 27 October 1957, a very strange incident occurred: a local policeman, eager to help his team, stood very close to the corner flag. When a corner was taken by the visitors, the officer deliberately positioned himself to prevent the Mexican player from running enough to deliver the ball. The player demanded he move, but the

policeman stood firm. Faced with the persistence of the mischievous uniformed man, Mexican coach Ignacio Trelles left the bench, ran to the corner, and pushed the intruder aside. After the corner was taken, Trelles returned to his place on the bench. The policeman, frightened, took refuge in the stands and did not interfere again.

* When the Brazilian Sports Confederation (then in charge of the national football team) sent the list of its 22 players to FIFA, it forgot to assign each player a number. To sort out the mess and help the squad, Uruguayan Lorenzo Villizio, a member of the World Cup organising committee, decided to assign a number to each player without consulting any Brazilian officials, pressured by the looming deadline for this requirement. Thus, the starting goalkeeper, Gilmar, was given three; midfielder Didí six; and defender Zózimo took nine. However, Villizio made an extraordinary move: he gave the number ten to a 17-year-old boy named Edson Arantes do Nacimento, who was known by his nickname, Pelé. The unusual thing about this case is that Pelé had played with the number 13 shirt in a friendly against Argentina, held a few months earlier, and usually played for his club, Santos, wearing eight or nine. From Sweden 1958 onwards number ten became synonymous with Pelé, and over the years, it has traditionally been the number of the most skilful player on every team.

* A ball called the Top Star, manufactured by the local company Sydsvenska Läder & Remfabriks, was used in Sweden. Its design consisted of 24 rectangular panels of yellow leather, interlaced in a zigzag pattern.

SWEDEN 1958

* On 8 June, at the Malmö Stadion, defending champions West Germany lined up to meet Argentina for the opening match. Upon noticing the two teams' kits, English referee Reginald Leafe thought the white of the German jersey could be mistaken for the light blue and white stripes of Argentina, especially since both teams wore black shorts and socks. Leafe called the two captains and by tossing a coin determined that Argentina would use an alternative kit. Since the South Americans didn't have another set of shirts, they accepted a loan from an official of IFK Malmö, the city's other club and traditional rivals of FF, whose stadium was being used. Thus, for the first time in their history, Argentina wore yellow shirts. And it was the last time, as they lost 3-1 and that colour was never used again.

* The meeting between Brazil and England on 11 June at Gothenburg's Ullevi Stadium broke an incredible streak: up to that point, every match in the first five World Cups had had at least one goal. This was the first goalless draw, after 115 games.

* Another series, albeit a disastrous one, was also broken on 11 June. In a 1-1 draw with Wales at Solna's Råsunda Stadium, with a goal scored in the 89th minute Mexico ended an astonishing streak of defeats that had plagued the team since the 1930 World Cup. They had lost each of their matches in 1930 (against France, Chile, and Argentina), 1950 (against Brazil, Yugoslavia, and Switzerland), and 1954 (against Brazil and France), in addition to their first match in Sweden, 3-0 against the host nation. Many fans attribute the end of the losing streak to the

change in the colour of their kit: in Sweden, Mexico debuted their now traditional green jersey, while in previous tournaments they had worn a maroon one. Another interesting fact was that the scorer of the goal against Wales, left-winger Jaime Belmonte, was known from that day on by a lavish nickname, 'The Hero of Solna'.

* 'Accustomed to always losing, getting a point in the World Cup seemed fabulous,' said Mexican defender Jorge Romo, who played in his team's draw with Wales.

* On 15 June in Gothenburg, Brazil defeated the Soviet Union 2-0, with two goals from Edvaldo Neto, known as Vavá. That day saw a surprising debut: Pelé played his first World Cup match at 17 years and 235 days old. This record would stand for 24 years, until Northern Ireland's Norman Whiteside faced Yugoslavia at the age of 17 years and 41 days, on 17 June 1982 in Spain.

* After drawing 2-2 with West Germany on 11 June at the Olympiastadion in Helsingborg, the Czechoslovakians complained about the refereeing of Englishman Arthur Ellis. They claimed that the judge had awarded a goal to the Germans when the score was 2-0 to Czechoslovakia, even though the ball had not crossed the line. The central Europeans' anger increased when they learned that Ellis would officiate the crucial match against Argentina, which both teams had to win to advance to the next round. A Czech official presented the tournament organisers with a video of the previous game, in which it was evident that West Germany's first goal had indeed been wrongly approved. However, FIFA rejected the

protest and retained Ellis for the decisive game, on 15 June, also at the Olympiastadion. In response, Czechoslovakia announced they would play 'under protest'. But on the pitch they soon forgot about the referee. Forty minutes into the first half they were already leading 3-0, and in the second half they handed Argentina their worst World Cup defeat: 6-1. Ellis, evidently, harboured no ill will toward the Czechs.

* Goal difference was still not used for the first phase. This meant that three of the four groups were settled with an extra match, as on each occasion two teams were tied on three points. In Group 1, Northern Ireland – with a goal difference of -1 – were 2-1 winners against Czechoslovakia, who had reached +4 following a 6-1 thrashing of Argentina. In Group 3, Wales (0) defeated Hungary (+3) 2-1. In Group 4, the Soviet Union (0) defeated England (0) 1-0.

* A few weeks before the start of the competition, the Northern Ireland Football Association requested that FIFA not schedule its matches on Sundays. The curious demand was based on the fact that six members of the squad – William Simpson, Sammy McCrory, Robert Rea, Sammy Chapman, Tommy Hamill and Robert Trainor – were devout Christians and strictly observed the biblical seventh-day rest. The players had been warned that two of the three first-round matches – against West Germany and Czechoslovakia – had been scheduled for Sundays. FIFA rejected the request, and Northern Ireland travelled to Sweden with only 16 players; the other six preferred to stay behind so as not to miss religious services at a Belfast church. The most curious thing

about this is that Northern Ireland didn't lose either of their Sunday matches: on 8 June they beat Czechoslovakia 1-0, and seven days later they drew 2-2 with West Germany. However, they lost 3-1 to Argentina on 11 June, a Wednesday, and were eliminated on the 19th, a Thursday, after losing 4-0 to France.

* Eight days after his debut, Pelé reached a record that remains in place at the time of publication. On 19 June, in the quarter-finals, Brazil beat Wales 1-0 at Ullevi. The only goal was scored by the brilliant young star, who was just 17 years and 239 days old – the youngest World Cup scorer.

* When the two semi-finals ended – Sweden defeated West Germany 3-0, while Brazil triumphed 5-2 over France – the tournament organisers discovered that both finalists were wearing yellow jerseys. A draw was held, which the South Americans lost. Because the Brazilians had no alternative jerseys, the team's kit manager had to go out and buy a new uniform, with one condition: no white, a colour banned since *El Maracanazo*. After a long tour of various Stockholm stores, the man acquired 20 blue shirts. Over two days he sewed the numbers on the backs and the Brazilian Sports Confederation's crests on the chest. The Swedish delegates were convinced that wearing yellow gave their team 'a decisive advantage', with one saying, 'There's a favourable psychological factor: there's always the possibility that an opposing player will make the mistake of passing the ball to one of our players.'

* On 28 June, France defeated West Germany 6-3 in the third-place match. Four of their goals were made

by Just Fontaine, who scored 13 times in a single tournament, a record still standing. Fontaine – who had travelled as a substitute and joined the squad due to an injury suffered by starting centre-forward Raymond Blair – scored goals in all six matches: three against Paraguay, two against Yugoslavia, one against Scotland, two against Northern Ireland, one against Brazil, and four against Germany. With his 'poker' in the final game, the French striker joined the exclusive list that included only Hungary's Sándor Kocsis, Poland's Ernest Wilimowski, and Brazil's Ademir.

* At the end of the tournament, a Swedish newspaper presented Just Fontaine with a rifle as a reward for being the top scorer.

* Despite competing wearing their unusual blue jerseys, Brazil crushed Sweden 5-2 in the first World Cup Final featuring two teams from different continents. Two goals from Pelé, two from Vavá, and one from Mário Zagallo made up the massive scoreline, which would never be repeated: no other team has to date managed to score five or more goals in the final of a World Cup. Furthermore, thanks to Sweden's two goals, the 1958 final went down in history as the highest-scoring decisive game. Brazil also became the first team to be crowned champions outside of their own continent.

* 'After they scored their fifth goal, I didn't feel like scoring them any more. I just wanted to applaud,' said Swedish defender Sigvard Parling, fascinated by the football Brazil displayed in the 1958 final.

* Two of the scorers in the 1958 final achieved records that are still in place: Pelé became the youngest player

to win a World Cup and also to score in a final, at 17 years and 237 days old, while Sweden's Nils Liedholm, scorer of one of the home team's goals, became the oldest player to score in a final, at 35 years and 263 days old.

* After receiving the Jules Rimet Trophy, Brazil's captain, centre-back Hilderaldo Bellini, raised it with both hands, at the request of the photographers surrounding him on the field who wanted to take a picture of him and the prize. The image went around the world, and since then, it has become a tradition for the captain of a winning team to raise the trophy after collecting it.

* For winning the World Cup, a television factory in Rio de Janeiro donated 23 sets free of charge, one for each player and one for the coach, Vicente Feola. Furthermore, just 24 hours after Brazil won the tournament, the Rio de Janeiro newspaper *Gaceta Sportiva* collected some 500,000 cruzeiros from its readers to reward the champions. By the time the heroes arrived home, the figure had risen to one million. Meanwhile, Brazilian president Juscelino Kubitschek de Oliveira signed a decree granting a pension to the players and their families. An exorbitant prize that demonstrated how much the world title was desired.

* 'I scored two goals in the World Cup Final. I became a champion. The [Swedish] king came to hug me and praise me. These things don't usually happen to a 17-year-old boy,' said the phenomenal Pelé, recalling the 1958 final several years later.

Statistical focus – teams that have scored the most World Cup goals:

Country	Goals	Tournaments
Brazil	237	22
Germany	232	20
Argentina	152	18
France	136	16
Italy	128	18

CHILE 1962

* At the FIFA Congress held on 10 June 1956, in Lisbon, two nations submitted their bids to host the seventh World Cup: Argentina and Chile. The president of the Argentine Football Association, Raúl Colombo, concluded a two-hour speech with a pedantry phrase, 'We can host the World Cup tomorrow. We have everything.' His counterpart from the Chilean federation, Carlos Dittborn, more humble and sensible, spoke for only 15 minutes and concluded his speech with a historic promise, 'Because we have nothing, we will do everything.' Chile won by a landslide, 32 votes to 10. The Andean country did, in fact, complete the necessary infrastructure projects for the World Cup on time. Dittborn, however, was unable to enjoy the tournament: he died a month before it began due to a heart attack, aged only 41.

* The absence of hosts Chile and holders Brazil from the 1962 South American qualifiers led to a very peculiar fixture list: six of the region's teams – Argentina, Ecuador, Uruguay, Peru, Colombia, and Bolivia – faced off in home-and-away matches in a series designed specifically to favour the qualification of countries bordering or closest to the host nation. Paraguay, the seventh South American entrants, played a one-on-one with the winner of the CONCACAF zone, Mexico. Why was the qualification determined by a random selection of

matches? Two years before the start of the World Cup, an earthquake severely affected four of the planned host cities – Talca, Concepción, Talcahuano, and Valdivia – restricting the tournament to another four venues: Arica, Rancagua, Viña del Mar, and Santiago. CONMEBOL agreed to manipulate the qualifying round to encourage the arrival of fans from neighbouring towns, whose money could help recoup the multi-million-dollar investment in stadium renovations and other expenses. But the operation didn't go well: Colombia defeated Peru, Uruguay beat Bolivia, and Mexico eliminated Paraguay. The only neighbouring team that fulfilled their mission were Argentina, who easily defeated Ecuador.

* Teams from Africa and Asia were clearly disadvantaged in the qualifying stage: without fixed spots, the continental winners had to face European teams in play-offs, who easily defeated them. Morocco, who had beaten Ghana and Tunisia, were eliminated after losing to Spain. South Korea, who had beaten Japan, lost in the intercontinental play-off to Yugoslavia. Thus, the 1962 World Cup featured five teams from South America, ten from Europe, and one from CONCACAF, Mexico.

* This was the first World Cup to use goal difference in the initial phase, determining qualification to the second round without the need to schedule play-off matches.

* For this tournament, FIFA approved the use of a ball manufactured by a Chilean company called Zamora. It was made of 18 leather panels – 12 hexagonal and six rectangular – dyed yellow, and had a name worthy of the world's top sporting event: Crack.

* When he arrived at the Santiago de Chile airport, Soviet referee Nikolaj Latychev discovered, to his dismay, that his suitcase had been lost at one of the airports where he had to change planes during his long journey from Moscow. Before leaving for the city of Rancagua, where he was to referee England v Argentina on 2 June, Latychev had to buy a new kit, and also a whistle, because the one he used in matches had been left in his missing luggage.

* West Germany coach Sepp Herberger, who had led the 1954 winners and also the squad that had finished fourth in Sweden in 1958, introduced a report card for each player. The brochure included 'subjects' such as technique, tactics, speed, discipline, hygiene, punctuality, and politeness, and Herberger, weekly, filled out each column with grades from one to ten. The novel evaluation system served little purpose: for the first time under Herberger, West Germany were eliminated in the quarter-finals, by Yugoslavia.

* For several days before the opening match against Brazil on 30 May at the Sausalito Stadium in Viña del Mar, Mexico coach Ignacio Trelles urged his defenders, Jesús del Muro, Guillermo Sepúlveda, and José Villegas, to concentrate throughout the game. In every training session, Trelles repeatedly stressed to the members of the back line that in order to avoid losing to the reigning champions it was crucial not to make any mistakes. Any blooper, he insisted endlessly, would prove fatal against forwards of the calibre of Garrincha, Pelé or Vavá. The repeated warnings paid off in the first half, which ended 0-0. But in the 56th minute Villegas naively lost the ball,

CHILE 1962

Pelé captured it, and sent a precise cross for Mário Zagallo's head and the scoring was opened. The goal devastated Villegas. Trelles noticed: he stood up from his seat on the bench and, standing next to the sideline, began encouraging his player to regain his composure. But, as the rules of the time dictated, an observer forced the coach to return to his seat. Trelles refused to give up. Noticing that Villegas wasn't recovering, he resorted to an extreme measure: he asked a Mexican newspaper reporter for his camera and, pretending to be a press worker, moved a few metres on to the field to calm the defender. The Brazilian players noticed the manoeuvre and alerted the referee, Switzerland's Gottfried Dienst, who sent the coach off. A few minutes later, Pelé took advantage of Villegas's confusion to score the second and decisive goal. Brazil won 2-0, and Villegas never played again in the World Cup.

* Due to the large number of injured players in various matches, some due to episodes of extreme violence, the Chilean tournament was dubbed the 'Hospital World Cup'. According to newspaper reports, during the first phase around 50 players were affected by various injuries, including five fractures, and were forced to withdraw from the competition.

* During Brazil's second match, against Czechoslovakia in Viña del Mar, on 2 June, Pelé hit a powerful shot that bounced off a post. The effort cost Pelé a tear that forced him to withdraw from the tournament. However, that afternoon, the outstanding Brazilian remained on the field until the end, limping due to the injury. The match ended 0-0, and the two teams would meet again in the final.

* Also on 2 June, at the National Stadium in Santiago, Chile and Italy faced each other in Group 2 – which they shared with Germany and Switzerland – in a very violent match. Seven minutes in, English referee Ken Aston ordered the expulsion of Italy's Giorgio Ferrini for punching Honorino Landa in the face. Ferrini refused to leave the field until a group of police officers forcibly removed him. A few minutes later, Landa himself savagely kicked an opponent, but Aston did not send him off. The official also did not penalise a punch by Chile striker Leonel Sánchez on Mario David. However, he did send off Italy's David in the 41st minute of the first half, when he got revenge on Sánchez with a terrible kick. Chile, with 11 players against nine Italians, won 2-0 in the second half and qualified for the second round.

* In their first World Cup appearance, Colombia lost 2-1 to Uruguay and 5-0 to Yugoslavia in the group stage, both at the Estadio Carlos Dittborn – a tribute to the director who had secured Chile's hosting of the tournament – in the city of Arica. At that same stadium, on 3 June, Colombia faced the Soviet Union and 11 minutes into the first half the South Americans were losing 3-0; 11 minutes into the second half it was 4-1. However, the Colombians refused to give up and achieved a miraculous 4-4 draw. Several Latin American newspapers joked about the acronym CCCP embroidered on the chest of the Soviet shirt, stating that, in Spanish, it meant *'Con Colombia Casi Perdemos'* (We Almost Lost Against Colombia).

* On 6 June, the Soviet Union and Uruguay faced each other in Arica, confident that the winner

would advance to the second round. Before the first half ended, with the Soviets leading 1-0 thanks to a goal from Aleksei Mamykin, Uruguayan midfielder Eliseo Álvarez collided with an opponent. At half-time, team doctor Roberto Masliah examined Álvarez and determined that he had suffered a broken leg. Masliah recommended that the injured defender not return to the field, but Álvarez, aware that Uruguay would have a difficult time turning the score around with a man fewer as substitutions were still not permitted, refused and ordered the doctor to apply a special bandage to immobilise the affected area. He returned to the game and completed the full 90 minutes limping and suffering excruciating pain, in yet another example of the *garra charrúa* ('charrúa's courage', in Spanish). In the 54th minute, Uruguay equalised thanks to José Sasía, but Álvarez's efforts weren't rewarded as they deserved: in the 89th minute, Valentín Ivanov scored the goal that qualified the Soviets for the second round and ended the South Americans' hopes.

* On 7 June at the Sausalito Stadium in Viña del Mar, Czechoslovakia stunned Mexico. After the whistle by Swiss ref Gottfried Dienst to start the match, the Mexican team moved and Guillermo Sepúlveda immediately lost the ball. The Czechs launched a lightning counter-attack that culminated with Václav Mašek's left-footed shot into the net. This goal, scored 15 seconds in, became the fastest World Cup goal for 40 years, until the 2002 edition in South Korea and Japan.

* During the quarter-final between Brazil and England on 10 June in Viña del Mar, a small dog

entered the pitch. The players and some police officers tried in vain to capture the intruder, until England's Jimmy Greaves got down on all fours and, slowly approaching, managed to catch the puppy and hand it over to an officer. However, the little animal didn't give up and, before being sent off, urinated on Greaves's chest. The striker had to continue the match surrounded by an unpleasant and stinking odour because there was no spare shirt available.

* 'For four years, we prepared our boys to face football teams. We didn't expect a player like Garrincha,' said England coach Walter Winterbottom after his team lost 3-1 to Brazil.

* Also on 10 June in the quarter-finals, at the Estadio Carlos Dittborn, Chile drew 1-1 with the Soviet Union, who had won the European Championship at the Parc des Princes in Paris two years earlier and were considered one of the favourites to win the World Cup. In the 29th minute, Chilean midfielder Eladio Rojas received a pass from a team-mate and unleashed a right-footed shot that travelled 30 yards and powerfully entered the net. Seeing that his missile had become a goal, Rojas ran the same 30 yards the ball had travelled and hugged the Soviet goalkeeper. After the match ended, with Chile winning 2-1, a journalist asked the hometown hero why he had celebrated his hit in such a manner. Rojas responded that he was moved by having beaten his idol, goalkeeper Lev Yashin, who would win the Ballon d'Or the following year.

* Believe it or not, before the semi-final against Brazil, the Chilean Football Association urged its fans not to shout 'too loudly' in the stadium because 'it

could upset our team emotionally'. It added, 'The championship is entering a phase in which the concentration of all physical strength is necessary to put on a good performance. We ask all of Chile, from the highest authorities to the closest relative, to keep the Chilean team within the structure of sporting preparation and emotional peace in which it is located. Everyone must sacrifice the pleasure of celebrating our players and put aside the shouts and hugs until Chile has finished its performance in the tournament.' The fans complied with the unusual directive, but Chile still lost 4-2 to Brazil.

* In the semi-final, Eladio Rojas, Chile's hero of the quarter-final against the Soviet Union, got into a fight with Brazilian star Garrincha. A few minutes before the end of the match between the two South American teams, with the *Verdeamarelos* leading 4-2, Rojas collapsed after being punched by Garrincha, who had scored two of Brazil's goals. On the recommendation of one of his linesmen, who witnessed the attack, Peruvian referee Arturo Yamasaki sent off the Brazilian forward. The result remained unchanged, and Brazil qualified for the final.

* 'I deeply regret what happened. It was an involuntary reaction on my part, probably as a result of some blows I had received in rough action. I was provoked and someone spat in my face, but that doesn't justify my reaction, and I want to apologise to the Chilean fans,' said Garrincha, minutes after the semi-final against Chile.

* Because Brazil had already lost Pelé to injury, the Brazilian Sports Confederation asked FIFA to

exempt Garrincha from being suspended for his dismissal against Chile and to allow him to play in the final. Although tournament regulations stipulated that sent-off players would have to serve a one-match suspension, FIFA – which was presided over by Englishman Stanley Rous – issued a statement three days before the final, announcing that the Brazilian star's expulsion had been overturned and that he was only cautioned for having hit Eladio Rojas, on the grounds that 'he always behaved well on the field'. Thus, Garrincha, who on the day of the final had the flu and a fever of 39 degrees, showed up to play against Czechoslovakia and, although he didn't score any goals, he led his team to a 3-1 victory and their second World Cup.

* In Chile, Brazil achieved four records: they won their second consecutive title and equalled Italy – champions in 1934 and 1938 – with a feat that has not since been repeated. Forward Vavá became the first player to score in two consecutive finals, a feat that only Frenchman Kylian Mbappé would match in Qatar 2022. The winning coach, Aymoré Moreira, was the brother of Alfredo Moreira, Brazil's coach at Switzerland 1954: the two are the only pair of brothers to have managed the same country's national team at different World Cups. Ultimately, Brazil became the champions who used the fewest players throughout a tournament: only 12. The only change came after Pelé was injured against Czechoslovakia in the first round. His place was taken by Amarildo.

* Czechoslovakia aren't the team who have lost the most World Cup finals without ever winning the trophy (the Netherlands lead that category, with

three unsuccessful outcomes), but they did achieve an unusual record: they lost the two finals they played, Italy 1934 and Chile 1962, despite leading 1-0 in both games.

* The 1962 World Cup in Chile ended with a very striking statistic: its top scorer was six different players, all with four goals! Never before had a World Cup had so many top scorers: Hungary's Flórián Albert, Brazil's Garrincha and Vavá, Chile's Leonel Sánchez, the Soviet Union's Valentín Ivanov and Yugoslavia's Dražan Jerković.

Statistical focus – teams that have conceded the most World Cup goals:

Country	Goals	Tournaments
Germany	130	20
Brazil	108	22
Mexico	101	17
Argentina	101	18
France	85	16

England 1966

* On Monday, 22 August 1960, three days before the start of the Rome Olympic Games, the FIFA Congress held at the elegant Albergo Quirinale awarded England the title of host of the eighth World Cup, scheduled for 1966, by 34 votes to 27 over West Germany. It is often said that the designation was made to celebrate the centenary of the founding of the Football Association, the governing body of the sport in England, and the drafting of the first version of the 'official' rules in 1866. However, both the institution and the statute had been born together – but in 1863.

* Fifteen African nations registered to participate in the qualifiers: Ghana, Sudan, Tunisia, Morocco, Ethiopia, the United Arab Republic (the official name of Egypt at the time), Guinea, Cameroon, Algeria, Senegal, Gabon, Libya, Liberia, Mali and Nigeria. However, upon learning that the winner of the continental zone would then play against the champion of the Asia/Oceania zone for a single spot across three continents, the 15 countries decided to boycott the tournament and refused to compete. They were right: European teams had nine spots available for only 30 nations.

* The withdrawal of the African teams helped North Korea's qualification; they only had to beat Australia in the group consisting of teams from Asia (South

Korea had entered, but later chose to withdraw) and Oceania.

* The biggest surprise of the European qualifiers was Portugal, who had never played in the World Cup. They competed against Czechoslovakia, the runners-up in the 1962 World Cup in Chile, along with Romania, and Turkey, and won Group 4, which granted them a direct ticket to England.

* A few months before the start of the 1966 World Cup, the trophy mysteriously disappeared from the windows of a London shop, where it was being displayed to promote the tournament. The enigmatic theft baffled the prestigious Scotland Yard police force, which, despite assigning the case to its best men, failed to obtain a single lead. The trophy was recovered by a collie dog named Pickles, who found it wrapped in newspapers in a garden in the London suburb of Beulah Hill.

* The 1966 World Cup inaugurated a charming custom: the selection of an official mascot, destined to be the symbol of the tournament. Mascots usually consist of a character design that describes the host nation through its clothing, fauna, or flora. The organisers chose World Cup Willie, a lion wearing a jersey with the Union Jack on its front.

* The official ball, the Challenge Four Stars, was made by the British firm Slazenger: it consisted of 25 leather panels, dyed orange.

* FIFA determined that if the quarter-finals and semi-finals ended level after 90 minutes and 30 minutes of extra time, they would be decided by a coin toss. For the final, however, it was determined that if the score

remained level after 120 minutes, the match would have to be replayed two days later. The coin toss was never used, and the final was decided in extra time. Doping controls were also implemented for the players to detect the use of prohibited substances. In this tournament, all the tests were negative.

* The opening match, England v Uruguay at Wembley, started with a significant delay due to seven of the English players leaving their identification at the hotel. To overcome the problem and prevent the home team from being forced to change their line-up, a member of the coaching staff asked a police officer to ride his motorcycle to the hotel, retrieve the forgotten identification, and return to Wembley. The officer managed to complete the task on time, despite the difficult traffic in the English capital. Thus, manager Alf Ramsey was able to continue with his starting line-up, which that day drew 0-0 against the tough South American team.

* Brazil included the youngest player in World Cup history: striker Edu was 16 years, 11 months, and six days old at the start of the tournament. However, the Santos striker did not appear in any of his team's three matches.

* On 12 July, at Goodison Park in Liverpool, Brazil defeated Bulgaria 2-0 with goals from Pelé and Garrincha. This was the last match for the *Verdeamarelo* team with its two famous stars on the field: that afternoon, Pelé received a violent kick from midfielder Dobromir Zhéchev, which kept him out of the match against Hungary on 15 July, at the same stadium. Brazil lost 3-1 to Hungary, and in that second match, Garrincha was also injured, missing the final

game against Portugal. Pelé, despite his injury, agreed to join the team that faced the Portuguese, but before the end of the first half he was forced to leave the field after a double tackle by defender João Morais which damaged his knee. The number ten played the second half with his knee bandaged, but could do nothing to prevent Portugal's 3-1 victory and Brazil's elimination. Pelé and Garrincha played 40 games together with the yellow and green jersey on, and were never defeated: the extraordinary duo totalled 36 wins and just four draws.

* Hungary's victory over Brazil also ended the longest unbeaten streak: until that day, Brazil had gone 13 matches without defeat, dating back to their first game at the 1958 World Cup in Sweden. They accumulated six matches in the Swedish tournament, six in Chile, and one in England, against Bulgaria.

* No one celebrated England's 2-0 victory over Mexico on 16 July at Wembley like Italy's Ubaldo Campanella. Much more, even, than the Three Lions' fans. Why? Because this man, held in the Alpine prison of Aosta, escaped from the prison while the guards were watching the match, broadcast on television. Campanella, who was serving a sentence of four years and seven months for cigarette smuggling, took advantage of his guards' distraction and slipped out the prison's main gate unnoticed.

* On 19 July at Wembley, Uruguay and Mexico played out a goalless draw. The Mexicans' goalkeeper was Antonio 'La Tota' Carbajal, who had previously played in 1950 in Brazil, 1954 in Switzerland, 1958 in Sweden, and 1962 in Chile. In England, Carbajal became the first player to appear in five World Cups,

a record later matched by several other players. 'La Tota' played a total of 11 World Cup matches, with a record of one win, two draws, and eight losses.

* That same day at Middlesbrough's Ayresome Park, one of the biggest upsets in World Cup history took place: North Korea, participating in their first tournament, defeated Italy 1-0 and qualified for the second round, a feat that until then had never been achieved by a nation that wasn't from Europe or South America. Before arriving in England, the Koreans had spent two weeks in East Germany, where they devoted themselves entirely to physical training, without playing any practice matches. Once in England, the players were prohibited from drinking alcohol and smoking, and were only allowed to play chess as a pastime. During lunches and dinners, the head of the delegation played military anthems through the dining room's audio system. In Group 4, the Koreans achieved a miraculous second place after a defeat to the Soviet Union, a draw with Chile, and an unexpected victory against Italy, whose squad included such famous Serie A stars as Internazionale's Sandro Mazzola and Giacinto Facchetti, and AC Milan's Gianni Rivera. The only goal was scored by Pak Doo-ik, who was a corporal in the army, where he worked as a dentist. For scoring this admirable goal, Doo-ik was promoted to sergeant. Another hero for the Asian team was goalkeeper Lee Chan-myung, who against the Soviet Union went down in history as the youngest goalkeeper in the World Cup, at 19 years and 191 days old. The victory baffled even the North Korean officials, who had prematurely booked their tickets to return home for after the Italy match.

ENGLAND 1966

* Bulgaria's Ivan Vutsov achieved a negative record in England, becoming the player with the most own goals in the World Cup: he scored one against Portugal and another against Hungary. FIFA awarded the second to Ivan Davidov, although television footage clearly shows that the ball bounced off Vutsov before entering the Bulgarian net.

* Before the quarter-finals were played, delegates from Argentina and Uruguay complained that FIFA had appointed a German referee, Rudolf Kreitlein, for England v Argentina, and an Englishman, James Finney, for West Germany v Uruguay, raising suspicions that the matches were fixed. The protests were filed in a trash can. The FIFA president at the time was Englishman Stanley Rous.

* The match between England and Argentina, played on 23 July at Wembley, was characterised by intense play and constant interruptions due to 'arguments' between players from both teams and Rudolf Kreitlein. In reality, no one understood anyone else, as the language barrier prevented any possibility of dialogue. After 35 minutes, the referee sent off Argentina's captain, Antonio Rattín. 'He [Rattín] didn't say anything I could understand, but I could read what he was saying on his face,' Kreitlein said two days later in an interview with the *Daily Mail*. With an extra man, the hosts won 1-0 thanks to a header from Geoff Hurst in the 78th minute.

* 'As I walked [toward the dressing room after being sent off], the fans threw aerated chocolate at me, which was completely new to me. We weren't familiar with them yet. I opened the wrapper, chewed a little, and threw it back. I reached the corner of the field

and saw a small British flag flying over the corner posts. I twisted it all up in my hand. It seems they had run out of chocolates, because then they started throwing closed beer cans at me. So, I ran away to avoid one hitting me on the head,' Antonio Rattín said in an article published by Argentinian newspaper *La Nación* several decades later.

* According to FIFA, yellow and red cards were invented by former English referee Ken Aston after England v Argentina in the 1966 World Cup. While driving home from Wembley, Aston stopped at traffic lights on Kensington High Street. The lights gave him the idea of incorporating red and yellow cards, a universally known colour code.

* While England defeated Argentina with a German referee, Uruguay suffered under the officiating of Englishman James Finney at Sheffield Wednesday's Hillsborough stadium. West Germany won 4-0 after Finney sent off two South American players, Horacio Troche and Héctor Silva. Furthermore, the day after that game, a German newspaper published a photo of defender Karl-Heinz Schnellinger committing a clear handball inside the penalty area that would have earned Uruguay a penalty when the score was 1-0 to the Europeans. Some newspapers and magazines alleged a plot against the two South American teams, but nothing could be proven.

* North Korea's surprising victory over Italy looked like it might be replicated in their quarter-final with Portugal: 25 minutes into the game, played on 23 July at Goodison Park, the Koreans were leading 3-0. But the Portuguese didn't give up and won 5-3, with four goals from their star striker, Eusébio, known by

the nickname the 'Panther of Mozambique', as he was born in that south-east African nation. Eusébio became the fifth player to score four times in a World Cup match.

* At the start of the tournament, England's potential semi-final was scheduled to take place at Goodison Park. However, the venue was changed at the last minute at the request of the home team and they instead faced Portugal on 26 July at Wembley. The *Daily Telegraph* described the match as 'a classic good, fair, sporting game'. England won 2-1 thanks to a brace from Bobby Charlton. According to the *Telegraph* this match was so imbued with 'fair play' that, after the striker scored his second goal, he shook hands with a Portuguese player who approached to congratulate him!

* Portugal won the bronze medal by defeating the Soviet Union in the third-place play-off, held at Wembley on 28 July. Eusébio, the tournament's top scorer with nine goals, scored once in a 2-1 victory. The Soviet team's captain was the famous Lev Yashin, the only goalkeeper to win the Ballon d'Or, in 1963.

* The final between England and Germany took place on 30 July at Wembley. The 90 minutes ended 2-2 – Geoff Hurst and Martin Peters scored for the hosts, Helmut Haller and Wolfgang Weber for the Germans – so extra time was required. Eleven minutes into the first half of extra time, Hurst's shot hit the underside of the crossbar, landed on the goal line, and bounced away. Gottfried Dienst consulted Soviet linesman Tofik Bakhramov, who assured him that the ball had bounced behind the line, something that the

television images do not make clear. In 1995, a study conducted by Oxford University determined that the ball fell six centimetres short of completely crossing the line. Eleven years later, *Monday Night Football* on Sky Sports conducted a simulation to 'confirm' that it had indeed crossed the line completely. But that afternoon at Wembley, the Swiss referee relied on the testimony of his assistant to endorse the controversial goal, which was immediately dubbed 'the ghost goal' by the media around the world. Hurst scored again before the final whistle – he became the first player to score three times in a final, a feat only equalled by Frenchman Kylian Mbappé in Qatar 2022 – and England were crowned world champions for the first and so far only time.

* 'I sleep peacefully, I know the ball went in,' said Gottfried Dienst when asked about England's third goal.

* England became the second world champions to feature two brothers: Manchester United striker Bobby Charlton and Leeds United defender Jack Charlton.

Statistical focus – players with the most World Cup wins:

Player	Country	Wins
Pelé	Brazil	3 (1958, 1962, 1970)
Giuseppe Meazza	Italy	2 (1934, 1938)
Giovanni Ferrari	Italy	2 (1934, 1938)
Guido Masetti	Italy	2 (1934, 1938)
Eraldo Monzeglio	Italy	2 (1934, 1938)
Garrincha	Brazil	2 (1958, 1962)
Gilmar	Brazil	2 (1958, 1962)
Djalma Santos	Brazil	2 (1958, 1962)
Zózimo	Brazil	2 (1958, 1962)
Nilton Santos	Brazil	2 (1958, 1962)
Mauro Ramos	Brazil	2 (1958, 1962)
Zito	Brazil	2 (1958, 1962)
Didí	Brazil	2 (1958, 1962)
Mario Zagallo	Brazil	2 (1958, 1962)
Vavá	Brazil	2 (1958, 1962)
Pepe	Brazil	2 (1958, 1962)
Daniel Passarella	Argentina	2 (1978, 1986)
Cafú	Brazil	2 (1994, 2002)
Ronaldo	Brazil	2 (1994, 2002)

Mexico 1970

* Mexico won the vote to select the host country for the 1970 World Cup against a rival who had already lost twice: Argentina. At the FIFA Congress held during the Tokyo Olympics, the Mexican proposal beat the South Americans' one by 56 votes to 32.

* After the boycott by African teams in the preliminary phase of England 1966, FIFA determined that, for the first time, Africa would be allocated one of the 16 spots for the qualifiers, and that Asia would also be awarded its spot, although it would have to be determined jointly with Oceania. Europe, meanwhile, kept its nine places (although only eight were in contention, due to the direct qualification of England). Three were assigned to South America, and two to CONCACAF, one of them to the host country.

* The qualifying rounds produced several surprises: Portugal, third in the previous World Cup, ended up last in European Group 1, behind Romania, Greece, and Switzerland. The most striking aspect is that the Portuguese squad began the preliminary competition with a 3-0 victory over Romania, the only team to qualify from that quartet.

* In Africa, after Zambia and Sudan won their respective first-round legs against each other at home, both 4-2, FIFA ordered the Sudanese team to advance because they had played the second leg at

home. Meanwhile, Tunisia were eliminated without losing a single match. After defeating Algeria over two legs, the Tunisians drew all three matches against Morocco in Marseille, France. A coin toss prevented Tunisia from competing in Mexico. Morocco then secured their ticket after a tough final group against Sudan and Nigeria, despite a defeat to the latter.

* In South America, Argentina were eliminated in the qualifying rounds, something that had never happened before and has not happened since. They finished last in a group they shared with Peru, the qualifiers, and Bolivia, after losing both away matches, in Lima and La Paz, and drawing 2-2 with Peru at home, only securing one victory, at home to Bolivia.

* The qualifying match between El Salvador and Honduras, in the CONCACAF zone, sparked what is known in the history books as the 'Football War'. El Salvador's victory – in a third match, played on 27 June 1969 at Mexico's Azteca Stadium, after both teams had won at home – was exploited by Honduran dictator Oswaldo López Orellano, who blamed immigrants from the neighbouring country for the economic crisis his nation was experiencing. On 14 July, the Salvadoran army crossed the border to defend their compatriots, sparking a five-day war. After the conflict, El Salvador defeated Haiti in the final qualifying round and secured a spot in the World Cup.

* This World Cup marked the beginning of a legendary dynasty: the official Adidas ball. The Telstar Durlast ball – the same one that would be used four years later in West Germany – had 32 black and white

leather segments. This ball is the granddaddy of the Tango, Azteca, Etrusco, Jabulani, and Al Rihla, among others, which have been used since.

* Technological advances allowed most of this World Cup's matches to be broadcast live via satellite around the world. Furthermore, this tournament was the first to offer colour matches for home television.

* 1970 featured two major regulatory debuts: the yellow and red cards created by English referee Ken Aston, which had been tested two years earlier in another Mexican tournament; and allowing all teams to make two substitutions per match. The two new rules debuted in the opening game, played on 30 May at the Azteca Stadium, a 0-0 draw between Mexico and the Soviet Union. Visiting defender Evgeny Lovchev received the first yellow card in World Cup history, while his compatriot Anatoliy Puzach had the honour of being the first substitute, replacing Viktor Serebryanikov before the start of the second half.

* On 3 June at the Estadio Jalisco in Guadalajara, Brazil crushed Czechoslovakia 4-1. The *Verdeamarela* squad, coached by Mário Zagallo, presented a marvellous attacking system articulated by four 'number ten' players – Pelé, Gerson, Rivelino and Tostão, who also acted as a centre-forward – and a speedy and skilful striker, Jairzinho, who not only became the tournament's top scorer but also netted in every game his team played. Against Czechoslovakia, Jairzinho scored a brace, while Pelé and Rivelino each scored once.

* 'The only player we didn't mark was the opposing goalkeeper when he took a throw-in,' said Mário

Zagallo of his team's approach to keeping the opposition under wraps.

* In their second match, on 7 June at the Azteca Stadium, Mexico defeated El Salvador 4-0. The final goal, in the 83rd minute, was scored by Juan Ignacio Basaguren, the first substitute to score in the World Cup. Basaguren had replaced Horacio López Salgado in the 76th minute.

* Thanks to two wins – 4-0 over El Salvador and 2-1 against Belgium – and a goalless draw against the Soviet Union, Mexico finally made it through the first round of the World Cup, after 40 years and six failed attempts, in 1930, 1950, 1954, 1958, 1962 and 1966.

* England were leading West Germany 2-0 in the 67th minute of their quarter-final on 14 June in León. At that moment, manager Alf Ramsey brought on substitute Colin Bell to replace Bobby Charlton, intending to spare Charlton for the semi-final. Ramsey was confident his team would maintain their advantage and repeat their 1966 World Cup success. But while Bell waited for the ball to be played out of touch so he could come on, the Germans scored through Franz Beckenbauer. Shortly after, in the 81st minute, Ramsey removed the scorer of England's second goal, attacking midfielder Martin Peters, and introduced defender Norman Hunter. The move proved ineffective as a minute later Uwe Seeler equalised. The 90 minutes ended 2-2, and in extra time, West Germany took advantage of the absences of Charlton and Peters to score the decisive goal, by Gerd Müller – who wore the number 13 shirt in honour of his idol, Max Morlock, who had

worn that number at the 1954 World Cup. Ramsey paid for his overconfidence as his world champions were eliminated. The Germans celebrated their swift revenge after the final at Wembley.

* When FIFA appointed Israeli Abraham Klein to referee the quarter-final between Mexico and Italy at the Luis Dosal Coliseum in Toluca, the home team's officials protested: Klein had officiated Mexico's defeat to Japan in the 1968 Olympic Games. Hours later, as if by magic, the Israeli withdrew from the match because, supposedly, he was ill, and it was finally officiated by Switzerland's Ruedi Scheurer. The referee change did not favour Mexico at all as they suffered a resounding 4-1 defeat.

* For the first time in World Cup history, the four teams in the semi-finals had already won the trophy: Uruguay, Brazil, Italy and West Germany.

* The semi-final between Brazil and Uruguay was scheduled for 17 June at the Azteca Stadium in Mexico City. However, at the request of Brazil, it was moved to Guadalajara. Uruguay's doctor, Roberto Masliah, said, 'Our players lost five kilos during the [quarter-final] match against the Soviet Union. When we were planning an intense physical recovery with a well-thought-out programme, FIFA surprised us by deciding to make us travel to Guadalajara. This was detrimental to us because it disrupted our work.' With these advantages in their favour, the 'rested' Brazilians won 3-1 and reached the final.

* Italy's electrifying 4-3 victory over West Germany in the second semi-final at the Azteca on 17 June was dubbed the 'Match of the Century'. In fact, in 2007, *World Soccer* magazine considered it the

best match in the history of football. The *Azzurri* opened the scoring in the eighth minute: Roberto Boninsegna set up a move with Luigi Riva and, upon receiving the ball, unleashed a left-footed shot that curled just inside goalkeeper Sepp Maier's right-hand post. Just when Italy's victory seemed secure, Karl-Heinz Schnellinger equalised in the 90th minute with a low shot from the edge of the six-yard box. Despite the heat, the altitude, and the gruelling 90 minutes already played, extra time produced a dramatic outcome: Gerd Müller gave West Germany the lead in the 94th minute; Tarcisio Burgnich and Riva turned the score around for Italy in the 98th and 104th minutes; Müller levelled again in the 110th, and a minute later Gianni Rivera made it 4-3.

* On 21 June the Azteca Stadium was the scene of a magnificent final, in which the superb Brazilian team crushed Italy's defensive barrier with their showy football. Pelé, Gérson, Jairzinho and Carlos Alberto gave a spectacular performance that allowed them to defeat the Europeans 4-1 and for ever claim the Jules Rimet Trophy. Or, at least, for a few years: as recounted in the second chapter of this book, in 1983 the trophy was stolen and its gold reduced to ingots. What the thieves failed to melt was the eternal memory of that Brazil team, considered by many fans around the world to be the best side in World Cup history.

* With his goal against Italy, Pelé added his name to the select list of players to have scored in two different World Cup finals. The number ten, also known as 'The King', had already scored against Sweden in the

1958 final, equalling the record held until then only by his compatriot Vavá.

* 'Pat, how do you spell Pelé?'
  'Easy: G, O, D.'

Former footballers Malcolm Allison and Pat Crerand, commentators for the BBC at the 1970 World Cup.

Statistical focus – World Cup top scorers

Player	Country	Goals	Tournaments
Miroslav Klose	Germany	16	2002, 2006, 2010, 2014
Ronaldo	Brazil	15	1994, 1998, 2002, 2006
Gerd Müller	Germany	14	1970, 1974
Just Fontaine	France	13	1958
Lionel Messi	Argentina	13	2006, 2010, 2014, 2018, 2022

West Germany 1974

* Two decades after the end of the Second World War, the Federal Republic of Germany was elected to host the tenth World Cup. The most striking aspect of its designation was that at the FIFA Congress where its bid was approved – held on 6 July 1966 in London, a few days before the start of that year's tournament – the German federation enjoyed the support of Englishman Stanley Rous, who was FIFA president at the time. The official appointment took place at the Royal Garden Hotel in London, after the other nation hoping to host the tournament, Spain, decided to pull back and reschedule its bid for 1982. The Iberian federation withdrew after learning of Rous's support for West Germany.

* After the appearance of World Cup Willie and his friend Juanito (a boy wearing the traditional Mexican sombrero), the Germans decided that, for the first time, their mascot would not be one, but two: Tip and Tap, a pair of brothers who symbolised the unity of the two halves of Germany, divided after the end of the Second World War. By then, Saarland had already been returned by France to the western part of the country.

* Group 1 of the European qualifying round had to be settled with an extra match, despite the use of goal difference if teams finished on equal points. In truth, the matter turned out to be more complex

than that, because Sweden, Austria and Hungary finished tied on eight points in a very evenly matched group, in which Malta also competed. Sweden and Austria participated in a play-off after having also finished with equal goal difference of +7 after three wins, two draws, and one loss. Hungary, meanwhile, were eliminated with a +5 goal difference, despite not having lost a single match. On 27 November 1973, at the Parkstadion in Gelsenkirchen, Sweden defeated Austria 2-1 and qualified for the World Cup.

* Also eliminated despite not having lost a qualifying match were Belgium. They defeated Norway and Iceland twice, and drew both matches with the Netherlands, who would win the group by a superior goal difference: +22 to +12.

* Probably the biggest surprise of the European qualifying round was Poland, who eliminated England. The Three Lions failed to win any of their matches at Wembley: they drew 1-1 with the Poles and Wales, the third and last member of Group 5. Britain's representation in the World Cup went exclusively to Scotland, who won Group 6 against Czechoslovakia and Denmark.

* Chile booked their ticket to Germany after a 1-0 win – against no one! The strange situation has its explanation: the Chilean squads won South American Group 3 in which they only faced Peru after Venezuela withdrew. Then, after winning a play-off with the two teams having beaten each other 2-0 in their two matches, they were assigned to participate in an intercontinental play-off against the winner of European Group 9, the Soviet Union. On 26 September 1973 the first leg was held in

Moscow, which ended 0-0. The second leg was scheduled for 21 November at the National Stadium in Santiago, but, a few days before, the Soviet Union expressed its condemnation of the *coup d'état* against Chilean president Salvador Allende, a representative of the Socialist Party. The putsch was led by the fascist general Augusto Pinochet, two weeks before the match in Moscow. The Soviet government announced that its national team would not play at the National Stadium, which had served as a detention centre for political prisoners, and requested that the rematch be held at a neutral venue. FIFA rejected the protest, and the Europeans opted to withdraw from the competition. Although they had already qualified, on 21 November Chile took to the pitch at the National Stadium to perform a parody as extravagant as it was lamentable: playing against no one. After home referee Rafael Hormazábal blew his whistle, Sergio Ahumada replaced Francisco Valdés, and these two, along with Carlos Reinoso and Julio Crisosto, took the ball with short touches towards the penalty area, before Valdés sent the ball into the empty net. The incredible action was celebrated by some 15,000 people who had entered the stadium to witness the unusual antics.

* Zaire, in Africa, and Australia, in Asia and Oceania, qualified for the World Cup for the first time. Both teams had to face long qualifying rounds that required them to play 11 matches each.

* After Brazil claimed the Jules Rimet Trophy for ever, thanks to winning their third World Cup in Mexico in 1970, FIFA had to find a new trophy. To this end, a design competition was held, in which 53

projects were submitted. The design most popular to the executives was that of Italian sculptor Silvio Gazzaniga, who was commissioned to create the award. The prize represents two human figures holding up the Earth. It measures 36.8 centimetres tall and weighs 6.175 kilograms, five of which are 18-carat gold. The base includes two rings of malachite, a semi-precious stone. Unlike the Jules Rimet Trophy, the new World Cup can never be won outright. The winner of each competition is only awarded a replica, which they can keep in perpetuity.

* In 1974, FIFA introduced a rather confusing competition system, which would be repeated for the following edition: an initial phase with four groups of four teams, of which the top two advanced to two groups, also of four, with the essence of semi-finals. At this stage, after playing each other once, the group winners qualified for the final and the runners-up for the third-place match; the rest were eliminated.

* The group stage draw placed the host country of the World Cup, the Federal Republic of Germany (as represented on the pitch by West Germany), which occupied the western half of what is now Germany, and also the German Democratic Republic (GDR, represented on the pitch by East Germany), the eastern portion controlled by a socialist government politically linked to the Soviet Union, in Group 1. The match, held on 22 June at the Volksparkstadion in Hamburg, attracted the attention of the world's press: in the midst of the Cold War two siblings representing two completely different lifestyles clashed. The West Germans symbolised capitalist society; the GDR, the socialist world. West Germany

WEST GERMANY 1974

had already qualified, having defeated the other two members of the group, Australia and Chile; East Germany needed at least a point to reach the second round, having drawn with Chile. The team from the east won 1-0, with a goal from Jürgen Sparwasser, and the two squads, holding hands like mascots Tip and Tap, advanced together to the next stage.

* In this World Cup, Scotland became the first country to be eliminated from a World Cup without losing a single match. They were placed in Group 2 along with Brazil, Yugoslavia, and Zaire. Scotland drew 0-0 with Brazil, 1-1 with Yugoslavia, and defeated the Africans 2-0. As Brazil and Yugoslavia had also drawn against each other, and both had defeated Zaire (3-0 and 9-0, respectively), a three-way tie on four points resulted, and the group was decided on goal difference. Scotland were thus eliminated despite their unbeaten record.

* On 14 June at the Olympic Stadium in Berlin, West Germany were leading Chile 1-0 with a goal from Paul Breitner. In the 68th minute, South American striker Carlos Caszely launched a terrible kick at German defender Berti Vogts. Turkish referee Doğan Babacan reached into his pocket and took out his red card: thus, Caszely became the first player to be red-carded at a World Cup. With one man fewer, Chile were unable to overcome the hosts, and the match was played without a change in the score.

* When the Netherlands played their first match, on 15 June against Uruguay at the Niedersachsenstadion in Hannover, their star player Johan Cruyff – a talented midfielder who played for FC Barcelona

and had previously led the Dutch club Ajax to win three European Cups between 1971 and 1973 – wore a different orange jersey than his team-mates. Why? The squad's sportswear supplier was Adidas, but Cruyff was supported by Puma. These two companies, at the time the most important in their field worldwide, were born on the same street in the German city of Herzogenaurach, founded by two rival brothers, Rudolf and Adolf Dassler, respectively. Shortly before the start of the tournament, Cruyff threatened the Dutch Football Federation with not competing if he was forced to wear the official kit. The player believed that Puma paid him too much money for him to appear in television images and newspaper and magazine photos with the Adidas logo on his chest, shoulders, and arms. Therefore, against Uruguay and throughout the World Cup, he wore the official kit, but without the emblem on the chest and with only two of the three traditional stripes on the sleeves of the shirt and shorts.

* Following Italy's 3-1 victory over Haiti at Munich's Olympic Stadium on 15 June, Haiti's Ernst Jean-Joseph became the first player to be expelled from the World Cup for doping. Traces of ephedrine, a substance banned by FIFA, were found in Jean-Joseph's post-match urine sample.

* On 23 June at Dortmund's Westfalenstadion, the Netherlands thrashed Bulgaria 4-1. Johan Neeskens scored two of the goals from the penalty spot. Until that moment, no player had ever scored twice from a penalty in a single World Cup match.

* The 1974 World Cup was the first to feature Asian referees. The experience proved fruitless: Iran's

Jafar Namdar, in charge of Australia v Chile on 22 June at Berlin's Olympic Stadium, appeared very unsure, spending the entire 90 minutes consulting his linesmen, the experienced Arie van Gemert from the Netherlands and Vital Loraux of Belgium, about every decision. But Namdar's worst mistake was booking Australian defender Ray Richards twice – without showing him the corresponding red card. Two minutes after the second yellow card, Namdar was called by Loraux, who pointed out his mistake and urged him to send off Richards. Despite this poor performance, Namdar was called on by FIFA to participate in another match at this World Cup, as a linesman in the third-place play-off between Brazil and Poland.

* After losing to Poland and drawing with Italy, Argentina had to thrash Haiti and hope that the Poles would defeat the Italians. On 22 June, the day before the two Group 4 matches were played, an Argentine journalist asked Polish striker Robert Gadocha, 'How are you going to play against Italy?' The left-footed forward replied, 'That depends on the Argentines.' Without blushing, Gadocha was asking his South American colleagues for an 'incentive' to beat Italy. As soon as he found a pay phone, the journalist dialled the Days Inn hotel where the Argentine delegation was staying and passed on the message. The players met in a room and, after a brief analysis of the situation, decided to raise money for the Poles. In his book, *Simply Football*, Argentine former defender Enrique Wolff confessed, 'We scraped together 25,000 dollars and offered the money to them. As I say, we stimulated them with money from our own pockets, with the added problem that if we didn't win by three goals and they complied, we'd still have to pay the cash and go home.' Poland defeated Italy 2-1, and Argentina thrashed Haiti 4-1; both teams qualified for the second round.

* After the first round, the Netherlands entered semi-final Group A along with Argentina, Brazil, and East Germany. Their first opponents, on 26 June at the Parkstadion in Gelsenkirchen, were Argentina. Coincidentally, the Dutch and Argentines had faced each other in a pre-World Cup friendly in Amsterdam. That day, the *Oranje*, led by Johan Cruyff, crushed their visitors 4-1, although the thrashing could have been more significant because the quality and speed of the Europeans surpassed the capabilities of the South Americans. 'The result is false, I want revenge,' Víctor Rodríguez, one of the triumvirate of coaches of the Argentine team, insolently protested to the press shortly afterwards. Generous fate granted Rodríguez the necessary revenge a month later, in the World Cup. However, the Netherlands once more humiliated Argentina, this time 4-0. The insolent Rodríguez did not speak to the press again.

* The difference between the Netherlands and Argentina on the pitch was so immense that, with the score at 2-0, South American goalkeeper Daniel Carnevali tried to rush in to take a free kick. 'Kid, don't worry,' ordered his captain, Roberto Perfumo. 'But, Roberto, we're losing 2-0!' Carnevali questioned. 'We're only in the first half. If we keep going like this, we'll be ten goals behind, man,' Perfumo argued.

WEST GERMANY 1974

* The press dubbed the Dutch display 'total football' due to the mobility of their players and their ability to switch roles and occupy every space on the field. The Netherlands secured first place in semi-final Group A and qualified for the final after three clean sheets. In their first six matches, they had not conceded a goal scored by an opposing player. In the first round they defeated Uruguay 2-0, drew 0-0 with Sweden, and defeated Bulgaria 4-1. In the second round, they won all three matches: 4-0 over Argentina and 2-0 against East Germany and Brazil. The only goal, for Bulgaria, was scored by a Dutchman: Ruud Krol scored an own goal.

* West Germany, meanwhile, also qualified for the final after defeating all three of their semi-final group opponents: Yugoslavia 2-0, Sweden 4-2 and Poland 1-0.

* The 1974 final, held at the Olympic Stadium in Munich, started late: the stadium staff had forgotten to place the flags in the corners of the pitch. Furthermore, this became the first World Cup Final not to be played in the host country's capital city, which at the time was Bonn.

* The Netherlands took the lead before any German players had touched the ball. They kicked off and passed the ball back and forth 15 times until Johan Cruyff, who had outpaced Berti Vogts, his personal marker, was brought down inside the penalty area by Uli Hoeneß. Johan Neeskens converted the penalty awarded by English referee Jack Taylor. His goal, scored in the 87th second, is the earliest in any World Cup Final.

* As had happened 20 years earlier in Switzerland, West Germany displayed their perseverance and

self-respect to overturn the deficit and become champions, with goals from Paul Breitner and Gerd Müller, both before the end of the first half. In the second half, saves from Sepp Maier and a defence led by a brilliant captain, Franz Beckenbauer, helped seal the victory for coach Helmut Schön's team.

* 'Cruyff was the better player, but I was a world champion,' said Franz Beckenbauer.

* The confident Dutch government ordered the Royal Post Office to print a series of stamps commemorating the national team's participation in the World Cup in West Germany. But the day after the final, the postal service had to destroy 100,000 stamps bearing the inscription 'Netherlands World Cup Champion'.

* 'Winning a World Cup is something that stays with you for ever,' said Rainer Bonhof, a player who was part of Germany's 1974 World Cup-winning team.

Statistical focus – players with the most World Cup appearances:

Player	Country	Appearances	Tournaments
Lionel Messi	Argentina	26	2006, 2010, 2014, 2018, 2022
Lothar Matthäus	Germany	25	1982, 1986, 1990, 1994, 1998
Miroslav Klose	Germany	24	2002, 2006, 2010, 2014
Paolo Maldini	Italy	23	1990, 1994, 1998, 2002
Cristiano Ronaldo	Portugal	22	2006, 2010, 2014, 2018, 2022

Argentina 1978

* After failed bids for the 1938, 1962 and 1970 tournaments, it was finally Argentina's turn in 1978. Its nomination had been confirmed on 6 July 1966 in London, during the FIFA Congress held at the Royal Garden Hotel, which also awarded the 1974 World Cup to the Federal Republic of Germany. Two years before the tournament's opening, a group of military officers overthrew president Isabel Martínez de Perón and anointed Lieutenant General Jorge Videla as the new head of the executive branch. Thus, the World Cup was held in a country governed by a dictatorship.

* 'I pray to God our Lord that this event may truly be a contribution to affirming peace. That peace we all desire for the whole world and for all people of the world,' said Jorge Videla in his opening speech at the 1978 World Cup.

* In this tournament, the last with only 16 teams, the unequal distribution of places among the various continental confederations intensified. While the European group, with 31 teams, claimed ten of the spots (Hungary defeated Bolivia in an intercontinental play-off), Africa only obtained one for its 26 teams, which went to Tunisia. In the CONCACAF zone, Haiti won ten matches, drew three, and lost only one, but didn't qualify. France, on the other hand, went to Argentina after only two wins, one draw, and one loss.

* The power of money was evident when Wales faced Scotland on 12 October 1977. Wales, who had used Wrexham's Racecourse Ground – with a capacity of 18,000 – to defeat Czechoslovakia 3-0 seven months earlier, chose to travel to England to host the Tartan Army. Aware that the Scots would be accompanied by thousands of fans, as a victory would see them qualify for Argentina, Welsh officials petitioned UEFA to change the venue for the momentous match. The organisation accepted the request, and the game was moved to Liverpool's Anfield stadium. In front of 51,000 spectators, Scotland defeated Wales 3-0 and booked their ticket to South America. The Welsh officials weren't too disappointed: they returned home with triple the money they would have raised in Wrexham.

* After two absences, in Mexico 1970 and Germany 1974, Spain managed to return to the World Cup finals after a very tough match. Literally. After beating Romania, Spain and Yugoslavia reached the final game of European Group 8, played on 30 November 1977 in Belgrade with a chance of travelling to the World Cup. A win, a draw, and even a narrow defeat favoured the visitors. However, *La Roja* had a terrible time, battling it out and being saved by the goalposts, until in the 70th minute, Argentina-born Rubén Cano scored the only goal of the match to take Spain to his homeland. Shortly after, Juanito was replaced by Daniel Ruiz-Bazán. As he left the field, the Andalusian striker made a mocking gesture to the crowd, which unleashed a shower of glass bottles, one of which shattered on his head. Unconscious, the assaulted player had to be taken off on a stretcher. Upon returning to Madrid,

ARGENTINA 1978

his head bandaged, the controversial striker stated that the blow 'was worth it, because we played the toughest game in recent years. We never flinched and we always stood up for it.' In his case, his face and his head.

* To prepare his team, Argentine coach César Menotti had pre-selected 25 players. Ten days before the tournament began, he had to determine the three names he would leave off the official list. Menotti opted to drop Humberto Bravo, Víctor Bottaniz, and Diego Maradona, a 17-year-old Argentinos Juniors youth player who had just scored three goals in training that same morning. Forty years after the difficult decision, Menotti acknowledged in an interview, 'If you asked me now if I was wrong, I would say "yes, maybe",' although he emphasised that questions over his decision were masked by Argentina winning the World Cup.

* In this tournament, FIFA maintained the system from four years earlier: a first phase with four groups of four teams; the top two advanced to two semi-final groups, of which the winners qualified for the final, and the runners-up for the bronze medal match. Likewise, Adidas presented for the first time a ball named after a distinctive element of the host country, in this case one of its traditional dances: Tango.

* Johan Cruyff, a star for the Netherlands in 1974, refused to play in Argentina. Although there was speculation for many years that he did not want to travel to a country ruled by a military dictatorship, Cruyff himself explained his reasons in a 2008 interview with an Argentine newspaper, 'My decision wasn't political. Not at all. It was a sporting decision,

because I felt I was at the end of my career. I didn't feel like giving my all, and therefore I shouldn't be there.'

* Only one of the 88 Latin American players at the World Cup, from Argentina, Brazil, Mexico, and Peru, was playing his club football in Europe: the hosts' Mario Kempes, who played for Valencia in Spain.

* On 1 June 1978, at the Monumental Stadium in Buenos Aires, West Germany and Poland played in the opening match, a 0-0 Group 2 draw. This scoreline was the fourth consecutive such instance, as the three first games of previous World Cups also ended goalless: England v Uruguay in 1966, Mexico v the Soviet Union in 1970, and Brazil v Yugoslavia in 1974.

* One day later, at the Estadio Gigante de Arroyito in Rosario, Tunisia defeated Mexico 3-1, becoming the first African team to win a World Cup match. Until then, Egypt (1934), Morocco (1970), and Zaire (1974) had all performed unsuccessfully.

* On 3 June, in Mar del Plata, Brazil and Sweden were drawing 1-1 in the opening match of Group 3. Seconds from the end, a corner was awarded to Brazil: Nelinho placed the ball next to the flag, took a run, and, at 90 minutes and six seconds, launched a cross that, an instant later, talented midfielder Zico sent to the goal with a precise header. But, at the same moment the ball reached the net, Welsh referee Clive Thomas blew his whistle and began waving his arms to indicate that the goal had not been allowed. While the Swedes celebrated the draw, the Brazilians demanded an explanation for an unusual decision: Thomas had finished the match with the ball in the

air. The referee stood firm, and the South American players left the field hurling insults. The next day, Friedrich Seipelt, a member of the FIFA referees' committee, informed Thomas that he was going home. He never officiated in the World Cup again.

* Three days later, Germany crushed Mexico. With the score 3-0, Mexican goalkeeper Pilar Reyes collided with the powerful German striker Karl-Heinz Rummenigge and suffered a cut on his right leg. Reyes had to leave the match and received 16 stitches in the dressing room, while his replacement, Pedro Soto, took his place. After Syrian referee Farouk Bouzo blew the final whistle, Soto entered the dressing room and found Reyes and his bloodied leg. Still suffering from the intense pain, the injured goalkeeper asked Soto how the match had ended. 'We tied it, Pilar,' his replacement responded. 'They scored three against you and three against me.' Mexico had lost 6-0.

* On 11 June, back in Mar del Plata, France and Hungary took to the field dressed in white to close out their Group 1 campaign, having been eliminated by Italy and Argentina. Due to an error in FIFA's official communication, which understood that the blue of the French national team and the red of the Hungarian squad could be confused on the black and white televisions of the time, the teams were asked to wear their change kits, which were the same colour. Because both sides had left the rest of their equipment in Buenos Aires, the problem was resolved when a manager from the Mar del Plata club Kimberley offered to lend a full set of green and white jerseys. Brazilian referee Arnaldo Coelho drew

lots with the captains, and France were assigned to wear the provided shirts. Thus, 'Kimberley' won a World Cup match 3-1.

* France set a World Cup record, perhaps an unsatisfactory one. In their three matches in the initial phase, they used all 22 players from their squad, including their three goalkeepers: Dominique Baratelli, Jean-Paul Bertrand-Demanes and Dominique Dropsy.

* Also on 11 June, the Netherlands, who had already qualified for the semi-final groups, closed out their first-phase games with a 3-2 defeat to Scotland. The first goal of the match, scored by Dutchman Rob Rensenbrink from a penalty, was the 1,000th goal of the World Cup. Rensenbrink was rewarded with watches, hams, a suit, and other gifts.

* Dick Nanninga was the first substitute to be sent off in a World Cup game. The incident occurred on 18 June at the Estadio Chateau Carreras in Córdoba, during the Netherlands–West Germany match in Group A of the second phase. Nanninga had replaced Piet Wildschut in the 79th minute – nine minutes later the Dutchman received a red card from Uruguayan referee Ramón Barreto after two fouls.

* After West Germany's 3-2 second-round defeat to Austria in Córdoba, coach Helmut Schön left his position with a record that remains in place today – 25 matches in charge of the same team. Schön guided West Germany in 1966, 1970, 1974 and 1978.

* Following the first round, Argentina – second in Group 1, after two wins over Hungary and France and a defeat to Italy – had to travel from Buenos

ARGENTINA 1978

Aires to Rosario to compete in the Group B of the second phase. Upon arriving at their accommodation, at the Rosario Central sports complex, coach César Menotti called aside attacking midfielder Mario Kempes, who had sported a luxuriant moustache throughout the first round. 'Mario, why don't you shave it off, and see if your luck changes?' Menotti asked, pointing out that, without a moustache, Kempes had been crowned top scorer in a tournament twice in Argentina, with Rosario Central, and twice in Spain, with Valencia. Two hours before the first match of the second round, against Poland, Kempes shaved his facial hair. With a clear face, he scored both goals in the 2-0 victory and, at the end of the tournament, he established himself as the World Cup's leading scorer with six goals.

* The most controversial match of this World Cup was between Argentina and Peru in the second phase. The home team won 6-0 and qualified for the final against the Netherlands, forcing Brazil to play the third-place match. The thrashing raised suspicions of bribery by the Argentine military government of Peruvian players. The two matches that closed Group A of the second phase, Austria v Germany and Netherlands v Italy, were played at the same time; in Group B, Brazil v Poland kicked off at 4.45pm in Mendoza and Argentina v Peru at 7.15pm in Rosario. When Brazil closed out their campaign with five points from three matches and a goal difference of +5, Argentina knew they had to defeat Peru by four goals to reach the final. Some media outlets reported that Argentine-born Peru goalkeeper Ramón Quiroga received money in exchange for allowing himself to be beaten. However, Quiroga continued to play for

his country, including in the 1981 qualifiers and the 1982 World Cup in Spain. Another telling fact is that, when the match was 0-0, visiting striker Juan José Muñante shot against one of Argentine goalkeeper Ubaldo Fillol's posts. In any case, no journalistic investigation ever presented irrefutable evidence of the alleged bribery. No Peruvian player was ever accused, by name, of having acted dishonestly.

* 'I believe in the integrity and honour of my players. What happened was that we played against an opponent who desperately needed to win and never stopped shooting at goal,' said Peruvian coach Marcos Calderón after his team's thrashing by Argentina.

* On 25 June, Argentina defeated the Netherlands 3-1 at the Monumental Stadium in Buenos Aires and won the World Cup for the first time. The 90 minutes ended 1-1, and for the third occasion the World Cup Final had to go to extra time. Mario Kempes, who scored twice against the Netherlands, became the first player to wear the 'triple crown': he was on the winning team, the top scorer with six goals, and was voted the tournament's best player.

* 'Everyone says Argentina bought the World Cup [in 1978]; they didn't buy anything, because in football, nobody buys anybody,' said João Havelange, FIFA president from 1974 to 1998, of the controversy over the hosts' progress to the final.

Statistical focus – youngest players to score a World Cup goal:

Player	Country	Age	Tournament
Pelé	Brazil	17 years, 239 days	Sweden 1958
Manuel Rosas	Mexico	18 years, 93 days	Uruguay 1930
Gavi	Spain	18 years, 110 days	Qatar 2022
Michael Owen	England	18 years, 191 days	France 1998
Nicolae Kovács	Romania	18 years, 198 days	Uruguay 1930

Spain 1982

* Like Argentina, Spain managed to secure World Cup hosting rights after several setbacks. The designation, however, came with a requirement: submitting more stadiums than previous host nations after FIFA increased the number of participating teams from 16 to 24. The Spanish federation wasn't intimidated and went for more, offering the largest number of venues in the entire history of the World Cup: 17. The cities of Madrid (Santiago Bernabéu and Vicente Calderón), Barcelona (Camp Nou and Sarriá), and Seville (Benito Villamarín and Ramón Sánchez-Pizjuán) each submitted two stadiums. Alicante (José Rico Pérez), Bilbao (San Mamés), Elche (Nuevo Estadio), Gijón (El Molinón), La Coruña (Riazor), Málaga (La Rosaleda), Oviedo (Carlos Tartiere), Valencia (Luis Casanovas), Valladolid (José Zorrilla), Vigo (Balaídos), and Zaragoza (La Romareda) provided one each.

* To prepare for qualifying, the Colombian federation hired Argentine coach Carlos Bilardo. In addition to preparing his team to play against Uruguay and Peru in a triangular tournament, the coach hired a 'witch' named Beatriz Becerra, a woman from Cali believed to have supernatural powers, and took her to Bogotá's Estadio Nemesio Camacho El Campín minutes before the opening match against Peru. The alleged witch doctor entered the dressing room and performed supposed magical passes in

front of the players, intended to help them win. But Colombia only drew 1-1 with Peru and Becerra lost: Bilardo dismissed her as soon as he returned to the dressing room.

* On 27 September 1980, the Bežigrad Stadium in Ljubljana – now the capital of Slovenia, but then the metropolis of the then-tangled Yugoslavia – was the scene of an unprecedented event: Dragan Pantelić scored the first goal by a goalkeeper in the World Cup. While no goalkeeper has scored in the finals, Pantelić started a string of goals in the qualifiers that were followed by other gloved heroes, such as Paraguay's José Luis Chilavert and Venezuela's Rafael Dudamel. The Serbian scored a penalty against Denmark, which not only contributed to his team's 2-1 win: at the end of the qualifying phase, that victory was key to Yugoslavia securing their ticket to the World Cup.

* The increase in participating teams favoured the CONCACAF and African federations, and the zone shared by Asia and Oceania, which increased their quotas by 100 per cent. Honduras and El Salvador qualified through the first federation, Algeria and Cameroon through the African route, and Kuwait and New Zealand through Asia and Oceania. Europe also benefited from a significant increase to 13 places, plus the host country's quota. South America increased its number from two to three, plus champions Argentina.

* In addition to the increase in the number of participants, the competition system was modified once again: six groups of four teams were formed, from which the top two teams qualified, forming

another four groups of three. The winner of each group qualified for the semi-finals. At that knockout stage, meanwhile, penalty shoot-outs were incorporated into the tournament for the first time to decide drawn matches.

* When the World Cup began in Spain on 13 June, Argentina and the United Kingdom were engaged in the Malvinas/Falklands War. On 2 April 1982, the leaders of the Argentine military dictatorship ordered the invasion of the archipelago, located approximately 500km (310 miles) east of Patagonia, which had been a British overseas territory since the mid-19th century. The UK responded with its military might, and a confrontation ensued that resulted in more than 900 deaths and 2,000 injuries. The war ended on 14 June when Argentine troops surrendered, the day after their national team's defeat by Belgium in the opening match. In this tournament, the UK had three participating teams: England, Scotland, and Northern Ireland. Fortunately, Argentina did not cross paths with any of them.

* 'Those were extremely difficult months, because the conflict brought the two countries I loved face to face: the one where I was born and the one that adopted me,' said Argentine midfielder Osvaldo Ardiles, who played in England for Tottenham Hotspur while the Malvinas/Falklands War was taking place.

* On 15 June, at the Nuevo Estadio in Elche, the biggest hammering in World Cup history took place: Hungary defeated El Salvador 10-1. László Kiss, who came on in the 55th minute for András Törőcsik, became the first substitute to score three goals in a single match. Incredibly, despite this achievement,

Hungary failed to advance past the first round, losing to Argentina and drawing with Belgium.

* When Northern Ireland met Yugoslavia on 17 June at La Romareda Stadium in Zaragoza, Norman Whiteside inscribed his name in World Cup history: at 17 years and 41 days old, Whiteside became the youngest player to feature in a World Cup game. His record still stood at the end of Qatar 2022.

* A day later, during the 1-1 draw between Italy and Peru at the Balaídos Stadium in Vigo, the burly Peruvian defender José Velásquez accidentally knocked down referee Walter Eschweiler. The German had a hard time getting up from the pitch and continuing his work, which caught the attention of the spectators. When a group of journalists returned to their hotel, where Eschweiler was also staying, and told a staff member what had happened to him, the woman responded, 'Man! Before the match, during lunch, [Eschweiler] drank no less than three litres of wine by himself.'

* When France scored their fourth goal against Kuwait, 80 minutes into the match on 21 June at the José Zorrilla Coliseum in Valladolid, Sheikh Fahad Al-Ahmed Al-Jaber Al-Sabah – the president of his country's football federation and Olympic Committee, as well as brother of the head of state of the small but oil-rich country – entered the field with his bodyguards to demand that Ukrainian referee Miroslav Stupar disallow the goal because, supposedly, a whistle in the stands had confused the Kuwaiti players. Several accounts reported by the press claimed that Al-Sabah even threatened the unarmed Stupar with his dagger. Frightened, the

referee obeyed: he disallowed the goal and ordered a dropped ball to restart the match, which nevertheless ended 4-1 because France scored another goal in the final minute.

* Algeria's surprise 2-1 victory over West Germany at El Molinón in Gijón revolutionised Group 2 and generated one of the most embarrassing episodes in World Cup history. On 24 June, Algeria closed out their campaign with a 3-2 win over Chile – who lost all their matches – and ended up with four points, having lost to Austria, the fourth-placed team in the group. The following day, when Germany (two points) and Austria (four) took to the field for the final group match, the standings indicated that a 1-0 German victory would qualify both European teams and eliminate the Africans. And so it happened: ten minutes in, Horst Hrubesch scored the only goal of the game. From then on, the two teams began passing the ball far outside their penalty areas, revealing an obvious collusion. The arrangement was so crude that a Gijón newspaper published its sports report in the police section. The German newspaper *Bild* headlined 'We're through, but what a shame'. Another daily, *Der Spiegel*, noted, 'Germany and Austria mocked the crowd.' Starting with the next World Cup, FIFA began scheduling the last two matches in each group on the same day and at the same time.

* 'At half-time, we decided to keep the 1-0 score because it was enough for us to qualify.' Austrian coach Georg Schmidt gave an unusual excuse during the press conference after the disgraceful match against Germany.

SPAIN 1982

* To face Poland in the first match of the second phase, on 28 June at the Camp Nou in Barcelona, Belgian coach Guy Thys included 37-year-old midfielder Wilfried Van Moer, who had already appeared in a World Cup – Mexico in 1970. What's remarkable about Van Moer is that he competed in his second World Cup after recovering from four fractures throughout his career.

* On 5 July, at Barcelona's Sarriá Stadium, Italy and Brazil played the best match of the tournament. The two teams contended in the final game of Group C in the second phase, having both defeated Argentina. Italy won 3-2 in a fast-paced, back-and-forth duel that featured moments of superb football. The three *Azzurri* goals were scored by Paolo Rossi, a striker who had been suspended for two years for his alleged involvement in match-fixing at the request of the mafia that controlled the illegal sports betting industry. Rossi's suspension was completed two months before the World Cup, and although he had been expected to miss the finals, coach Enzo Bearzot relied on him to build his attack.

* Paolo Rossi scored again, this time twice, in the semi-final against Poland – Italy's first opponents, with whom they had drawn 0-0 in Vigo – for a resounding 2-0 victory.

* In the other semi-final, on 8 July at the Ramón Sánchez-Pizjuán Stadium in Seville, France were leading West Germany 3-1 in extra time (the first 90 minutes had ended 1-1) but the men in white miraculously equalised thanks to two goals from Karl-Heinz Rummenigge and Klaus Fischer, with a spectacular bicycle kick. The 3-3 draw led to the first

World Cup penalty shoot-out, which Germany won 5-4 thanks to two saves by their goalkeeper, Harald Schumacher. Of course, Schumacher shouldn't have been there: in the 60th minute he brought down Patrick Battiston with a violent blow inside the German penalty area, while the Frenchman was leading a dizzying and dangerous counter-attack. Dutch referee Charles Corver neither called a foul nor sent off Schumacher, although Battiston, unconscious from the terrible impact, had to be taken by ambulance to a nearby hospital.

* In the final, played on 11 July at the Santiago Bernabéu Stadium in Madrid, Italy soundly defeated West Germany. Paolo Rossi – who became the tournament's top scorer with six goals – Marco Tardelli, and Alessandro Altobelli built an insurmountable 3-0 lead. Paul Breitner, author of the 'honour' goal in the 83rd minute, became the third player to score in two different World Cup finals. In the 25th minute, with the score still 0-0, Italian defender Antonio Cabrini fired a penalty wide, the only one missed in a final, excluding shoot-outs. *Azzurri* goalkeeper Dino Zoff became the oldest player to win the World Cup, at 40 years and four months old.

* Italian defender Claudio Gentile, born in the Libyan city of Tripoli, became the first African-born man to win the World Cup.

* 'God bless whoever invented football,' said Paolo Rossi.

Statistical focus – players with the most minutes played in the World Cup:

Player	Country	Minutes	Tournaments
Lionel Messi	Argentina	2,314	2006, 2010, 2014, 2018, 2022
Paolo Maldini	Italy	2,220	1990, 1994, 1998, 2002
Lothar Matthäus	Germany	2,045	1982, 1986, 1990, 1994, 1998
Uwe Seeler	Germany	1,980	1958, 1962, 1966, 1970
Javier Mascherano	Argentina	1,950	2006, 2010, 2014, 2018

MEXICO 1986

* The FIFA Congress held on 9 June 1974, in Frankfurt, Germany, designated Colombia as the host country for the 1986 World Cup. However, three months after the end of the 1982 tournament, Colombian president Belisario Betancur announced that his nation was not in a financially strong enough position. His admission was based on the fact that, when Colombia registered its bid, the World Cup was to be played by 16 teams, but with the increase to 24 participants following Spain 1982, ten large stadiums were needed, and Colombia did not have them. CONCACAF president Joaquín Soria Terrazas subsequently nominated Mexico, which had already hosted the tournament 12 years earlier, to compete alongside the United States and Canada. Mexico was anointed at the FIFA Congress held on 19 May 1983, in Stockholm, and became the first country to host two World Cups.

* In September 1985, less than a year before the start of the tournament, a powerful earthquake struck much of Mexico, especially its capital city. The violent tremor caused an estimated 10,000 deaths and destroyed hundreds of buildings and homes. The 12 stadiums designated for the World Cup were unscathed.

* During Argentina's 3-1 qualifying victory over Colombia on 2 June 1985, at El Campín in Bogotá,

MEXICO 1986

Diego Maradona achieved something astonishing: he turned insults into applause. How so? In the middle of the match, he headed to one of the corners to take a kick. As he approached the stands, a spectator insulted him and threw an orange at him. Instead of getting angry and responding to the blasphemy, Diego stepped on the fruit, lifted it off the ground, and began to play keepie-uppie. Pure talent! Some witnesses counted 21 touches, but beyond that number, Diego, with his enormous skill, earned the ovation of the entire crowd, including the fan who had tried to hit him with the orange.

* Seconds after Scotland drew 1-1 with Wales at Ninian Park in Cardiff on 10 September 1985, and qualified for the intercontinental play-off against Australia, visiting coach Jock Stein, overcome with emotion, clutched his chest and fell next to the substitutes' bench. Stein was lifted by his players and carried to a stretcher inside the dressing room, where he died minutes later. For the match against Australia, the Scottish FA hired young coach Alex Ferguson, who led the team to a 2-0 victory in Glasgow and a 0-0 draw in Melbourne that sealed qualification for Mexico.

* FIFA decided to change the competition system for the eighth time: six groups of four teams were divided. For the second round – a knockout stage starting with the last 16 – the top two teams from each group and the four best third-placed finishers took part.

* The 1986 World Cup was characterised by many excellent matches in the sweltering Mexican summer heat. As in 1970, most of the games were scheduled

for midday, in a very hot area, to favour European television audiences.

* In Group A of the initial round, Bulgaria reached the second stage for the first time, after four previous unsuccessful attempts. The unusual aspect is that they did so without a win: they drew with Italy and South Korea, and lost to Argentina.

* Following Spain's 2-1 Group D victory over Northern Ireland on 7 June in Jalisco, Guadalajara, Catalan forward Ramón Calderé's doping test came back positive. However, FIFA did not sanction the player: the prohibited substance found in Calderé's urine – ephedrine – corresponded to a medicine used to treat the flu. The drug had been reported on the official form by the Iberian team's doctor, Jorge Guillén. The Spanish federation paid a fine equivalent to 25,000 Swiss francs for Guillén's negligence, but Calderé was not suspended. After the match against Northern Ireland, he played against Algeria in the final group match, Denmark in the last 16, and Belgium in the quarter-final.

* On 8 June at the Estadio Neza 86, Uruguay suffered their worst World Cup defeat, losing 6-1 to Denmark. According to some media reports, the crushing loss was the result of a diarrhoea outbreak suffered by several players. A few days before the match, according to reports, the squad experienced the flare-up due to eating spoiled food.

* On 11 June, at the Bombonera stadium in Toluca, Paraguay's Cayetano Ré became the first coach to be sent off in a World Cup. The incident occurred after Roberto Cabañas levelled at 2-2 for the South Americans in the 76th minute against Belgium,

which qualified both teams for the second round. Ré, deeply upset by the performance of Bulgarian referee Bogdan Dotchev, unleashed a vicious insult. Dotchev, understandably, didn't understand the insult, but his Chilean linesman Hernán Silva Arce did, and immediately reported what had happened. Dotchev then approached the substitutes' bench and dismissed Ré.

* That same matchday, in Zapopan, an unprecedented event occurred: Morocco, who had drawn 0-0 with Poland and England, defeated Portugal 3-1 and became the first African team to win a World Cup group. The feat was achieved thanks to two goals from Abderrazak Khairi in the first half and another from Abdelkrim Merry in the second. Morocco also had excellent players such as goalkeeper Ezaki Badou and midfielder Aziz Bouderbala.

* Two days later, the Estadio Neza 86 was the scene of another red record: French referee Joel Quiniou sent off José Batista just 50 seconds after the kick-off! Uruguay and Scotland were playing their final group match. Just 38 seconds into the game, Batista kicked attacking midfielder Gordon Strachan to the ground. Quiniou approached the Uruguayan defender and, 12 seconds after the blow, issued a red card. Uruguay managed to keep the score at 0-0 and, thanks to that point, they qualified for the second round.

* At the ninth attempt, Mexico won a match at the second stage of the World Cup. In the last 16 on 15 June, at the Azteca Stadium in Mexico City, packed with 115,000 fans, they defeated Bulgaria 2-0 thanks to goals from Manuel Negrete and Raúl Servín.

* That same day, at the Estadio Nou Camp in León, Soviet player Igor Belanov – winner of that year's Ballon d'Or – scored three goals against Belgium. Unfortunately for the Ukrainian-born striker, the Soviets lost 4-3 and were eliminated from the tournament.

* Spain's Emilio Butragueño became the sixth player to score four goals in a World Cup match, when his team crushed Denmark 5-1 on 18 June at La Corregidora Stadium in Querétaro, to reach the quarter-finals.

* On 21 June, at the Estadio Jalisco in the quarter-finals, France defeated Brazil on penalties after a 1-1 draw. The match was thrilling due to the numerous chances for both teams; goalkeepers Joël Bats and Carlos Gallo excelled. The striking aspect of this match was that both number tens, Zico and Michel Platini, missed penalties: the Brazilian in the 74th minute, when the score was already 1-1; the Frenchman in the shoot-out, which his team still won 4-3 due to misses by Sócrates and Julio César.

* That same day, at the Estadio Universitario in Monterrey, Mexico and West Germany played out the first goalless draw in a World Cup knockout match. After two hours of play, the two teams faced off in a penalty shoot-out. The Germans converted all four of their attempts, while goalkeeper Harald Schumacher saved shots from Fernando Quirarte and Raúl Servín, which put them through to the semi-finals. Schumacher, meanwhile, became the first goalkeeper to save four penalties in World Cup shoot-outs: he had already saved two against France in the 1982 semi-final in Spain.

* A day later, the Azteca Stadium witnessed one of the most remarkable matches in the history of the World Cup. Not only because of the way the game played out, but because the clash between Argentina and England took place four years after the Malvinas/Falklands War, fought between the South American nation and the UK. 'This was revenge, it was about getting something back from the Malvinas ... All we could do was think about it, it wasn't just another game!' admitted the phenomenal Diego Maradona in his autobiography, *El Diego*. After a goalless first half, six minutes into the second period Maradona received the ball just yards from the centre circle. He eluded Glenn Hoddle, weaved through three other Englishmen, passed it to Jorge Valdano, and went for the return. Valdano's ball came up, and Steve Hodge tried to clear, but it went high and back, heading for Peter Shilton's six-yard box. Maradona, who was running in, went for the ball, leaped, and beat Shilton – with his hand. The goal was awarded by Tunisian referee Ali Bin Nasser. After the match, Diego said that it had been the work of 'the hand of God'. Four minutes later, Maradona once again displayed his magic on the Azteca grass, this time to score the greatest goal in World Cup history. He received a short pass from Héctor Enrique inside the Argentina half and took the ball, turned, and darted between Peter Reid and Peter Beardsley. Several strides later, he darted inside and evaded Terry Butcher, then he weaved outside again to avoid Terry Fenwick. When Shilton emerged, he feinted a shot, but also evaded the goalkeeper. He finished into an open goal. The marvellous dribble, which left more than half of the England team in confusion, was honoured by FIFA in 2000 as its 'Goal of the Century'. England reduced the deficit with a goal from Gary Lineker, but Argentina managed to hold on to their advantage, ultimately winning 2-1.

* 'If it hadn't been an important match, I would have applauded,' said Gary Lineker, who suffered and enjoyed Diego Maradona's extraordinary goal.

* The two semi-finals were played on the same day, 25 June, and both ended with the same score: 2-0. In Guadalajara, West Germany defeated the highly backed France. In Mexico City, meanwhile, Argentina beat Belgium with another brace from the brilliant Diego Maradona.

* The final, on 29 June at the Azteca Stadium, had an epic outcome: just 20 minutes from the end, Argentina were winning 2-0 with goals from José Luis Brown and Jorge Valdano. But, between the 73rd and 80th minutes West Germany scored twice. For the first, Andreas Brehme's corner from the left was headed down by Rudi Völler for Karl-Heinz Rummenigge to score. Then Thomas Berthold set up Völler who, also unmarked, guided the ball home with his head. Barely three minutes later, Maradona, with his blood hot and his brain cold, composed a first-class left-footed pass that set up Jorge Burruchaga. Burruchaga escaped all alone towards the German goal and, when Harald Schumacher came out, he slotted the ball to the far post to seal the final 3-2. Argentina earned their second star and the Germans lost their second consecutive final.

* While all the Argentine players were jubilantly celebrating in their dressing room after winning the world's top title, Carlos Bilardo continued to suffer as

a result of the two German goals. For the punctilious coach – famous for his obsession with taking free kicks, both in attack and defence – the two German goals, both from headers inside the six-yard box, were two sharp stabs that cut short his desire to celebrate the victory.

* In Mexico, Argentine goalkeeper Héctor Zelada became the eighth and last World Cup-winning footballer who never played for his national team, not even in a friendly. The other seven are Juan Carlos Calvo (Uruguay 1930), Giuseppe Cavanna (Italy 1934), Pietro Arcari (Italy 1934), Aldo Donati (Italy 1938), Bruno Chizzo (Italy 1938), Luis Alberto Rijo (Uruguay 1950) and Washington Ortuño (Uruguay 1950).

* 'Football doesn't solve anything; it doesn't lower the price of bread. I wish we could solve the country's problems by going to play in Mexico. I swear I'd stay there if necessary!' Diego Maradona spoke with brutal honesty upon returning home with the World Cup. At the time, Argentina was going through a severe economic crisis.

Statistical focus – players with appearances in the most World Cups:

Player	Country	Tournaments
Antonio Carbajal	Mexico	5 (1950, 1954, 1958, 1962, 1966)
Lothar Matthäus	Germany	5 (1982, 1986, 1990, 1994, 1998)
Rafael Márquez	Mexico	5 (2002, 2006, 2010, 2014, 2018)
Andrés Guardado	Mexico	5 (2006, 2010, 2014, 2018, 2022)
Lionel Messi	Argentina	5 (2006, 2010, 2014, 2018, 2022)
Cristiano Ronaldo	Portugal	5 (2006, 2010, 2014, 2018, 2022)

† Italy's Gianluigi Buffon and Mexico's Francisco Guillermo Ochoa were with their teams in five World Cups, but did not play in all of them.

Italy 1990

* Many European nations expressed interest in hosting the 1990 World Cup: Austria, England, France, Greece, Italy, the Soviet Union, West Germany, and Yugoslavia officially announced their bids when the stipulated deadline of 31 July 1983 arrived. However, as the months passed, six countries withdrew, and only two maintained their candidacies: Italy and the Soviet Union. On 19 May 1984, at the FIFA Congress held in Zurich, Italy won by 11 votes to 5, becoming the second nation to host the tournament twice.

* The European qualifying round featured a major surprise: France, who had finished third in Mexico, were shipwrecked in a qualifying group that, at first, seemed very friendly. *Les Bleus* failed to win away, losing to Scotland and Yugoslavia, and drawing with Norway and the weak Cyprus, and were eliminated in third place in Group 5, behind winners Yugoslavia and runners-up Scotland.

* The South American qualifying phase included a match that went down in history as one of the greatest scandals in sports. On 3 September 1989, at the historic Maracanã, Brazil and Chile were playing for a ticket to Italy. In the 67th minute, with the score 1-0 to the home team, visiting goalkeeper Roberto Rojas fell wounded, with a flare thrown from the stands next to him. Chilean medics treated

Rojas, who was taken off on a stretcher with blood on his face and shirt. The entire Chile squad then left the field to condemn the 'attack'. The match was suspended by Argentine referee Juan Carlos Loustau, and Chilean officials and players stated that they would appeal to FIFA for the points, a sanction for Brazil, and a spot at the World Cup. However, an investigation by the international federation, which included a photograph showing that the flare had fallen one metre from the goalkeeper and not on his head, determined that the visitors had staged a farce to obtain an off-field victory rather than one on the Maracanã pitch. Rojas's injuries were real, but had been caused by his own hand, which had cut his eyebrow with a small scalpel hidden in one of his gloves. Everything went wrong for the Chilean federation: the match was awarded to Brazil, they were fined 100,000 Swiss francs, and banned from qualifying for the following World Cup. Rojas was also given a lifetime ban from playing.

* Meanwhile, in the CONCACAF region, Mexico were banned due to a sanction imposed by FIFA. In the preliminary tournament for the 1989 Under-20 World Cup in Saudi Arabia, held in Guatemala in April 1988, Mexico fielded four players in their starting line-up who were over the age limit of 19: one 20, two 22, and one 24. The fraud, known as 'the case of the *cachirules*' (in Mexico, an illegitimate child is called a *cachirul*), was discovered and reported by a journalist. FIFA banned Mexico for two years from all international competitions. During that time they lost their chance to qualify for a spot in Italy; the United States and Costa Rica took advantage, both reaching the World Cup for the first time.

ITALY 1990

* In the Asian group, South Korea and the United Arab Emirates qualified after participating in an intense six-team tournament that took place between 12 and 28 October 1989, at the National Stadium in Singapore. The two winners came out ahead of China, Qatar, Saudi Arabia, and North Korea. The UAE secured their first and so far only World Cup appearance.

* The 1990 tournament replicated the system used in Mexico, with six groups of four teams, the top two from each going through to the second round along with the four best third-placed finishers. The official match ball, named the Etrusco Unico by manufacturer Adidas, featured exquisite designs representing the culture of Ancient Rome.

* Italy 1990 is remembered for its famous official song, 'Un'estate italiana'. The ballad was composed by Italian musician Giorgio Moroder and originally had English lyrics written by Tom Whitlock, titled 'To Be Number One'. However, unhappy with the text, Moroder discarded the American's work and commissioned new lyrics from his compatriots Edoardo Bennato and Gianna Nannini, who at the time were two of the leading figures in Italian rock. The new version – also known as 'Magical Nights' ('Notti magiche') – became a huge hit and was for ever cemented among the top songs of the World Cup.

* On 7 June, the day before Argentina and Cameroon played the tournament's opening match, the South American country's president, Carlos Menem, who had travelled to Milan specially, gave Diego Maradona a diplomatic passport and named him

an honorary advisor to the government 'for sports affairs and the dissemination of Argentina's image abroad'. Maradona expressed his gratitude for the appointment, but several players, as well as some members of the coaching staff, cursed the absurd incident: Menem had a reputation for spreading bad luck. The following day, at the Giuseppe Meazza Stadium, the holders lost 1-0 to Cameroon. Diego also lost a diamond-studded hoop earring, valued at around 5,000 dollars, that his wife Claudia had given him on his previous birthday.

* 'Thanks to me, the Italians in Milan stopped being racist: today, for the first time, they supported the Africans,' said Diego Maradona at the end of the opening match. At the time, the Argentine captain was playing for Napoli, a club in southern Italy.

* Two days later, at the Stadio Renato Dall'Ara in Bologna, Colombia defeated the debuting United Arab Emirates 2-0, marking their first World Cup victory. Goals from Bernardo Redín and Carlos Valderrama secured a triumph that they had been denied in their only previous appearance, at Chile in 1962.

* On 13 June, Diego Maradona executed his second 'hand of God' moment. Against the Soviet Union, at the San Paolo Coliseum in Naples, Argentina got off to a very poor start: their goalkeeper, Nery Pumpido, fractured the tibia and fibula of his right leg after colliding with team-mate Julio Olarticoechea. The game restarted with Sergio Goycochea in goal and a corner for the Europeans. Igor Dobrovolski sent a cross to the front post, which was headed goalwards by Oleg Kuznetsov. The ball, which seemed destined

for the net, was cleared off the line by Maradona – with his right arm! A clear penalty that Swedish referee Erik Fredriksson didn't see, despite being standing less than two metres away from the action. Once the heat was over, Argentina managed to recover and defeat the Soviets 2-0.

* The following day, at Bari's Stadio San Nicola, the surprising Cameroonians defeated Romania 2-1 thanks to a double from Roger Milla, and became the first team to qualify for the second round. As suggested by several media outlets at the time, their remarkable performance was linked to the fact that the hotel was close to a safari-style zoo with free-roaming animals, which the players frequently visited. 'The atmosphere isn't African, but it helps you not miss your family or our landscape,' said defender Emmanuel Kundé when asked by a reporter.

* On 15 June, West Germany thrashed the United Arab Emirates 5-1. However, the happiest player of the day was Emirati Khalid Ismaïl, who scored the 'honour' goal for his team. For scoring the Emirates' first World Cup goal, a sheikh gave him a luxurious Rolls-Royce car.

* Ahead of facing Brazil on 16 June at the Stadio delle Alpi in Turin, Costa Rica abandoned their traditional red shirt to wear one designed with black and white vertical stripes. Why? Because with this kit, identical to that of stadium host club Juventus, they hoped to win the support of the Turin public. The change of attire served to gain the support of the fans of the 'Old Lady', but it failed to change Costa Rica's fortunes; Brazil won 1-0.

* Group F, which was played on the islands of Sicily and Sardinia, was very evenly matched: five games ended in draws and only one with a winner, England defeating Egypt 1-0 on 21 June at the Stadio di Cagliari. The Republic of Ireland and the Netherlands finished the first phase with the same number of points, goals scored and conceded: drawing lots placed the Irish in second place in the group and the Dutch in third. Both advanced to the next phase.

* Cameroon, after their wins over Argentina and Romania, lost 4-0 to the Soviet Union in their final group game. Thus, they became the first, and so far only, team to finish first in their group with a negative goal difference (-2) in World Cup history. Five days later, in a second-round match in Naples, Milla repeated his double against Colombia, and Cameroon became the first African team to reach the quarter-finals.

* On 24 June in Turin, Argentina, who had qualified third in their group with one win, one draw, and one loss, faced Brazil, who had arrived with three victories. Brazil had countless scoring opportunities, including three times hitting a post and several miraculous saves by goalkeeper Sergio Goycochea. However, in a counter-attack generated by Diego Maradona, Argentine striker Claudio Caniggia scored the only goal of the South American derby. Afterwards, Brazilian left-back Branco reported that, in the middle of the match, an Argentine team assistant offered him a plastic bottle containing an 'emetic' liquid, which made him nauseous and drowsy. Although this incident was never officially

clarified and was always denied by Argentine coach Carlos Bilardo, several *Albiceleste* players who had participated in that match, including Maradona, claimed to have been aware of it. 'Someone pulverised a Rohypnol [and put it into the water bottle] and everything went to hell,' Diego said on a television programme years later.

* The following day, the Republic of Ireland achieved an unprecedented record: they reached the World Cup quarter-finals without having won a single match. Englishman Jack Charlton's team drew 1-1 with England, 0-0 with Egypt and 1-1 with the Netherlands in the group stage. Then, in the last 16 at Genoa's Luigi Ferraris Stadium, they drew 0-0 with Romania after two hours of play, before winning 5-4 on penalties.

* The quarter-final between Argentina and Yugoslavia on 30 June in Florence also ended goalless and had to be settled by a penalty shoot-out that proved to be a true roller coaster of emotions. Argentina went 2-0 up after Dragan Stojković hit the crossbar. But after one Yugoslav goal, keeper Tomislav Ivković saved Diego Maradona's shot, and Pedro Troglio also hit the post. Things had become very difficult for Argentina, as the score was 2-2, and the South Americans had taken one penalty more. At that moment, something unusual happened: Faruk Hadžibegić entered the box, positioned the ball, and ran for a shot. However, Swiss referee Kurt Röthlisberger stopped him, pointing out that, according to the list provided by Yugoslavian coach Ivica Osim, the player due to take the fourth kick was actually Dragoljub Brnović. This mistake threw everyone off and was capitalised on by

Argentine goalkeeper Sergio Goycochea, the great hero of the afternoon, who saved Brnović's effort. Gustavo Dezotti then scored, and Goycochea kept out the final attempt by a nervous and unfocused Hadžibegić, and Argentina qualified for the semi-finals after a thrilling shoot-out that ended 3-2.

* That same day, at Rome's Stadio Olimpico, Italy ended Ireland's draw streak; the home team won 1-0 with a goal from Salvatore Schillaci.

* On 1 July in Naples, England and Cameroon played out the most thrilling encounter of the World Cup so far. The Three Lions opened the scoring in the 25th minute with a David Platt header. Emmanuel Kundé equalised in the second half with a penalty, and Eugène Ekéké doubled the lead by chipping the ball past goalkeeper Peter Shilton. But, just when a Cameroon victory seemed increasingly likely, Mexican referee Edgardo Codesal awarded a dubious penalty to England, which Gary Lineker converted into a goal. In extra time, Codesal called another foul inside the Cameroonian box, just as controversial as the previous one, allowing Lineker to secure England's 3-2 victory.

* As in Mexico 1986, the semi-finals were again played out with the same identical scoreline – in this case, 1-1 and 4-3 in the penalty shoot-out – and, once again, West Germany and Argentina qualified for the final: never before had two teams met twice in the World Cup Final. The Germans defeated England and Argentina saw off Italy. The Argentine goal, scored by Claudio Caniggia, ended goalkeeper Walter Zenga's unbeaten run, having gone 517 minutes without conceding a goal since the start of

the tournament. That record still stood by the end of Qatar 2022.

* On 8 July, at the Stadio Olimpico in Rome, West Germany, in their third consecutive World Cup Final, managed to break their losing streak by beating Argentina 1-0. The only goal of the game was scored by Andreas Brehme, a controversial penalty awarded by Edgardo Codesal, after Argentine defender Néstor Sensini fouled Rudi Völler inside the box. The referee's performance was heavily criticised by the Argentines, not only for the penalty: Codesal also sent off two Argentine players, Pedro Monzón and Gustavo Dezotti. Monzón became the first player to be sent off in a World Cup Final. Argentina also became the first team to fail to score in the final; up until that point, every team had managed to score at least once.

* West Germany coach Franz Beckenbauer equalled a feat that, until Italy 1990, had only been achieved by Brazil's Mário Zagallo, in becoming a World Cup winner as both a player and a coach; Beckenbauer had captained the victorious West Germans in 1974.

* The 1990 World Cup had a negative record: it was the tournament with the worst goalscoring average in history at 2.21 per match, resulting from 115 goals in 52 games. FIFA also noted that the ball spent more time in the goalkeepers' hands than on the pitch, so it implemented a rule change, prohibiting keepers from handling balls passed to them by team-mates with the feet.

Statistical focus – players with the most World Cup appearances as captain:

Player	Country	Appearances	As captain
Lionel Messi	Argentina	26	19
Diego Maradona	Argentina	21	16
Rafael Márquez†	Mexico	19	15
Cristiano Ronaldo	Portugal	21	14
Dino Zoff	Italy	17	14

†In Mexico, Márquez is credited with 17, but in two of those matches he did not appear as captain; Andrés Guardado gave him the armband upon leaving the field.

UNITED STATES 1994

* The election of the United States as the host of the 1994 World Cup was formalised on 4 July, the nation's Independence Day, in 1988, during a FIFA Congress held in Zurich. With ten votes, the US defeated Morocco, the first African country to bid to host the championship, which received seven. Brazil, seeking its second World Cup, received only two votes. The US designation was widely criticised because, in that nation, 'soccer' was not – and is still not – the most popular sport. Neither was it the second, nor the third. However, two very important factors weighed heavily within FIFA: first, that several powerful sponsoring companies of the international federation had their headquarters in the United States – among them, Coca-Cola, Mastercard, General Motors, and McDonald's – and secondly, the United States Soccer Federation committed to creating a professional league after the dissolution of the North American Soccer League in 1984. Thus, Major League Soccer was founded in 1993; its first tournament was held in 1996 with only ten teams.

* For this competition, FIFA decided to increase one spot for the African confederation, which had three participants: Cameroon, Morocco and Nigeria.

* England failed to qualify, after finishing third in their European group, behind the Netherlands

and Norway. They drew both matches at Wembley against the qualified teams, and also lost to both on the road. The day after the loss to the Dutch in Rotterdam, which meant England's elimination, the *News of the World* headlined 'End of the world'.

* France missed out for the second consecutive tournament. With a strong team led by the remarkable Eric Cantona, the French got off to a good start, and with only two matches remaining – both at the Parc des Princes in Paris – a simple draw was enough to secure their long-awaited qualification. On 13 October 1993 they hosted Israel, whom they had thrashed 4-0 in Tel Aviv; they were bottom of the group and already eliminated. The home team took a 2-1 lead, but the Israelis turned the score around with two goals in the 83rd and 93rd minutes. A month later, France took to the field to face Bulgaria. In the 90th minute, with the score 1-1 and Scottish referee Leslie Mottram holding his whistle to blow the final whistle as soon as the ball left the pitch, a 35-yard shot from Emil Kostadinov hit the corner of Bernard Lama's goal and went in. While the Bulgarians celebrated their qualification, the French left the field under a barrage of insults.

* On 11 October 1992, Ethiopia arrived in Casablanca with high hopes of a good result against Morocco in the opening match of African qualifying. But, as the minutes passed, the visiting squad began to lose players, stricken with severe diarrhoea that was reportedly caused by a lunch with spoiled food. The coach was forced to make the two permitted substitutions in just a few minutes, but the epidemic continued, and the Waliya Boyz continued to drop

UNITED STATES 1994

like flies. The match was suspended after 55 minutes, with the score 5-0 and only six Ethiopians on the field, one player short of the rules. The rest of the squad fought for a place on the dressing room toilets.

* In South America, the qualifying rounds offered surprises everywhere. In Group A, Colombia – coached by Francisco Maturana off the field and captained by Carlos Valderrama on it – secured their ticket to the United States with an extraordinary 5-0 victory over Argentina at the Monumental Stadium in Buenos Aires. Argentina quickly healed their wounds and also qualified, but after playing an intercontinental play-off against Australia, which included the return of Diego Maradona. The Mexico 1986 hero had not participated in the first round of qualifying due to an alleged dispute with coach Alfio Basile.

* In South America's Group B, Bolivia secured a place in the World Cup through qualifying for the first time; they had only participated in Uruguay in 1930 and Brazil in 1950 without pre-competition games due to the withdrawal of other teams. Bolivia qualified behind Brazil and ahead of Uruguay, Ecuador, and Venezuela thanks to winning all of their home matches in La Paz, a city located around 3,600 metres above sea level. Brazil were victims of the altitude, losing a qualifying match for the first time.

* For the first time in World Cup history, the tournament was held in stadiums that had essentially been built for other sports: Soldier Field in Chicago, the Cotton Bowl in Dallas, the Rose Bowl in Los Angeles, the Pontiac Silverdome in Detroit, the

Stanford Bowl in San Francisco, Giants Stadium in New Jersey, Foxboro in Boston, the Citrus Bowl in Orlando, and the Robert Kennedy Memorial in Washington were used primarily as venues for NFL games. All the stadiums had to replace their synthetic turf with natural grass, and in some cases – such as the Pontiac Silverdome – the substitutes' benches had to be moved into the stands because football fields are about 20 yards wider than those for NFL, and the sidelines were too close to the platforms.

* The opening party, held on 17 June at Soldier Field, offered a hilarious blooper to the 65,000 attendees and millions of television viewers watching the show: one of the guest artists, singer Diana Ross, was supposed to kick a ball toward a prop goal while singing a song. The choreography was set so that the plastic goal, upon being hit by the ball, would split in two, allowing Ross to run toward one of the stands. The distance between the ball and the goal was barely three metres. But, incredibly, she missed the shot, and the goal still collapsed anyway. Ross continued with her show, unperturbed, as if nothing unusual had happened. Her blunder, however, earned her a place in the 'top one' of World Cup opening extravaganzas.

* Two rules were introduced at this World Cup: three points for each victory in the group stage having previously always been two, and the players' last names (or nicknames) printed on the backs of their shirts.

* During the opening match, in which the unified Germany beat Bolivia 1-0 in Group C, the South Americans' Marco Etcheverry became the fastest

substitute to be sent off in a World Cup: Etcheverry entered the field in the 79th minute and three minutes later received a red card for kicking German defender Lothar Matthäus. Germany's victory broke a 24-year streak for world champions: the last holder to win in their first match at the following edition had been England, who beat Romania 1-0 in Mexico 1970.

* On 22 June at the Rose Bowl in Los Angeles, the United States defeated Colombia 2-1 in Group A. Colombia had lost their opening game to Romania and, after the second defeat, were eliminated from the World Cup. Defender Andrés Escobar scored the home team's first point with an own goal. Twenty days later, Escobar, who had returned to Medellín, where he lived and played for Atlético Nacional, was shot and killed by a man with whom, according to witnesses, he had argued over that fateful goal.

* Giants Stadium in New Jersey was the scene of an unusual event: on 23 June, Italy's Gianluca Pagliuca became the first goalkeeper to be sent off in a World Cup match. Pagliuca received a red card in the 21st minute after leaving his penalty area and kicking Norwegian midfielder Øyvind Leonhardsen, who was advancing alone towards the *Azzurri* goal. Needing to include Luca Marchegiani, the substitute goalkeeper, in the squad, coach Arrigo Sacchi made a very risky move: he took off his team's biggest star, Roberto Baggio. The situation had become complicated because Italy had lost their first match, against the Republic of Ireland in Group E, and a defeat would have practically eliminated them. However, the manoeuvre proved perfect, because,

despite playing almost an hour with one fewer player, Italy defeated Norway 1-0.

* The following day, in San Francisco, another record was set by a card: during the Group B match against Brazil, Cameroonian Rigobert Song became the youngest player to be sent off in the World Cup, aged just 17 years and 358 days old. Brazil took advantage and won 3-0.

* On 25 June, at Foxboro Stadium in Boston in a Group D match, Argentina defeated Nigeria 2-1, thanks to a brace from Claudio Caniggia. After the match, a nurse named Sue Carpenter entered the field and took Diego Maradona by the hand to guide him to the doping control room. A few hours later, FIFA announced that banned substances had been found in the urine sample taken from the Argentine captain. According to one report, an associate of Maradona's, who supplied him with vitamin, amino acid, and weight-loss pills, bought a fat burner containing ephedrine in the United States and, without realising that the tablets included this FIFA-banned substance, gave them to the number ten. Diego was expelled from the World Cup and banned from playing in official competitions for 15 months.

* In their second appearance, Bulgaria broke a record of ineffectiveness: on 26 June, at Soldier Field in Chicago, they got their first World Cup match win, beating Greece 4-0. Until then, they had only suffered 11 defeats and six draws in the 1962, 1966, 1970, 1974 and 1986 World Cups. At USA 1994 they had started with a 3-0 defeat to Nigeria.

* When they met on 28 June, Russia and Cameroon had already been eliminated, so the match was of no

UNITED STATES 1994

significance for Group B. But that day, at Stanford Stadium in San Francisco, two important World Cup records were broken, ones that still stood at the end of the Qatar 2022 edition: with his goal in the 46th minute, Roger Milla broke his own record from Italy 1990 as the oldest player, now aged 42 years and 39 days, to score in a World Cup. On the other team, forward Oleg Salenko scored five goals, a feat never achieved by any other player in a World Cup match. With six goals – he had scored another against Sweden – Salenko established himself as the tournament's top scorer after just three games played, although he had to share the title with Bulgarian Hristo Stoichkov.

* After all the matches in Group E had been played, there was an exceptional four-way tie between Mexico, Italy, the Republic of Ireland, and Norway. For the first and only time in the World Cup, all four teams won one match, drew one, and lost the other. Furthermore, all the teams achieved the same goal difference – zero – because the victories were achieved by the narrowest margin. Mexico topped the group with three goals scored and three conceded, Italy and Ireland advanced having scored and conceded twice each, and Norway with just a single entry in each column.

* Twenty minutes into the last-16 match between Mexico and Bulgaria, which ended 1-1 at Giants Stadium in New Jersey on 5 July, Mexican defender Marcelino Bernal dived over his own goal line to clear a shot. However, the action didn't finish there, as Bernal continued to run and ended his swift sprint trapped in the net. In addition to becoming a fish,

Bernal broke one of the goalposts. While the referee and players tried to fix the problem by tying the net to one of the television cranes, a team of stadium workers entered the field with a substitute goal and, within seconds, replaced the damaged setup with a new one. Once the incident was over, the match continued as normal. The score remained unchanged, and Bulgaria eliminated Mexico in a penalty shoot-out.

* Also on 5 July, at Foxboro Stadium, Italy's Gianfranco Zola suffered a bitter birthday: in the 76th minute, with his team losing 1-0 to Nigeria, Zola struggled with African defender Augustine Eguavoen, who collapsed to the grass. Mexican referee Arturo Brizio Carter mistakenly ruled that Zola had hit his opponent and sent the striker off with a straight red card. On his 28th birthday, Zola left the pitch in tears, but the day ended happily for him, as his teammate Roberto Baggio gave him two gifts: one in the 88th minute and another during extra time. Italy won 2-1, and Zola did not play again in the tournament. First, he had to serve a one-match suspension in the quarter-finals. Then Arrigo Sacchi decided not to include him in the semi-finals, nor in the final.

* Roberto Baggio returned to the scene and delivered at a crucial moment on 9 July in Boston, scoring in the 88th minute to make it 2-1, as Italy defeated Spain in the quarter-final. However, the *Azzurri*'s victory was tinged with red – and not by the Spanish kit, which that afternoon was white. In the third minute of stoppage time, with Spain fighting for an equaliser, Basque full-back Jon Andoni Goikoetxea launched a cross toward the Italian penalty area, which went

wide over the byline. In the box, striker Luis Enrique was left lying on his back after receiving a treacherous elbow from defender Mauro Tassotti. Luis Enrique got up with his face covered in blood, which was evidence of the Italian's malicious foul. Everything seemed to indicate that Hungarian referee Sándor Puhl would award a penalty and send Tassotti off. But neither Puhl nor his assistants saw what they were supposed to see. Italy won despite angry Spanish protests and the obvious evidence of foul play on Luis Enrique's face. Two days later, the FIFA Disciplinary Committee reviewed a video of the match to reconsider the incident, which was not included in the referee's report, and made a historic decision, as the organisation had never before used tape to study a case that occurred on the field of play: Tassotti was punished with an eight-match suspension and a fine of 20,000 Swiss francs. However, justice came too late for the Spanish, as they had already returned home eliminated. It was unclear why no punishment was applied to the distracted Puhl, much less why he was selected for the World Cup Final.

* For the first time in World Cup history, a final was decided by a penalty shoot-out. Italy – who had defeated Bulgaria in the semi-final with another Roberto Baggio brace – and Brazil, who crushed Sweden with a solitary goal from Rio de Janeiro native Romário, failed to put a ball in the net during the two-hour climax of the tournament. Brazil won 3-2 in the shoot-out, thanks to misses by Franco Baresi, Daniele Massaro, and Baggio, who had worn the hero's cape throughout the tournament – but forgot to put it on for the final.

* How does it feel to hold this trophy in my hands? Cold, it's frozen solid!' An admission from Romário, a standout figure in Brazil's victorious 1994 team.

* The 1994 World Cup set a surprising record: up to and including the 2022 tournament in Qatar, it is the tournament with the largest number of spectators in the stadiums. The 52 matches were attended by a total of 3.6 million fans, an average of nearly 69,000 per game. This achievement is striking because the second-placed tournament, Brazil 2014, drew 3,386,810 spectators, but in 64 matches, 12 more than those played on US soil.

Statistical focus – World Cups with the most goals

Tournament	Goals
Qatar 2022	172
Brazil 2014	171
France 1998	171
Russia 2018	169
South Korea and Japan 2002	161

These tournaments each had 64 games.

France 1998

* France became the third country to host the World Cup for the second time, announced at the FIFA Congress held in Zurich on 2 July 1992. France, which proposed ten venues and the construction of a new stadium in the Saint-Denis neighbourhood of Paris, defeated Morocco by 12 to 7.

* 'The system had to be changed. This is something we asked for, that FIFA should get away from embedded practices,' said Morocco's minister of sports, Abdellatif Semlali, who was deeply upset by his country's defeat to France at the FIFA Congress. Semlali's complaint did not fall on deaf ears: the next edition of the World Cup was played in South Korea and Japan, two Asian nations.

* For this edition, FIFA increased the number of participating countries from 24 to 32 and modified the system: the initial round consisted of eight groups of four teams each. The top two from each group qualified for the second phase, the knockout stage starting in the round of 16.

* In South America, CONMEBOL determined that, for the first time, the World Cup spots assigned to the region would be decided in a round-robin competition. Because Brazil had qualified directly as champions, FIFA awarded South America four direct spots, which went to Argentina, Paraguay, Colombia, and Chile.

* During the qualifying match between Bolivia and Argentina, played in La Paz on 2 April 1997, an unusual situation occurred: in the 88th minute, with the score 2-1 to the home team, and in a very heated atmosphere (Argentina had seen two players sent off), visiting forward Julio Cruz went to look for a ball hidden under the home bench. In the midst of the struggle, Cruz was hit in the right cheekbone by a Bolivian staff member. The match ended without any change in the score, and with the Argentines down to eight men: two dismissed and one knocked out. Minutes later, Argentina coach Daniel Passarella called in the photographers who had travelled from Buenos Aires to take dramatic pictures of Cruz, unconscious on a stretcher, his face covered in blood that had flown from a cut on his left cheekbone. How, if the punch had landed on the right side of the face? Apparently someone, using a sharp object, tried to amplify the striker's situation to claim the match points from CONMEBOL, but so clumsily that he slashed the wrong cheekbone! When he learned of the pathetic manoeuvre, Argentine Football Association president Julio Grondona ordered that no claims be made and that the wound, supposedly caused by the blow, be attributed to an injury caused by an imaginary stumble in the dressing room.

* In Europe, the continued dismemberment of nations like the Soviet Union and Yugoslavia increased the number of participating teams from 39 to 49. One of the surprises was Croatia, who secured their first World Cup qualification.

* In addition to Croatia, three other countries earned their first World Cup berths: Jamaica, who upset

Costa Rica in the final round of the CONCACAF group stage; South Africa, who took advantage of the significant increase in spots awarded by FIFA to the African continent, from three to five; and Japan, also benefiting from the expansion of spots for the Asian region, from two to three plus a possible fourth after a play-off with a team from the Oceania zone.

* In Asia, Iran qualified after winning a play-off against Australia, Oceania's representatives. However, before reaching that match, Iran got their record win to date in World Cup qualifying, crushing the Maldives 17-0 away on 2 June 1997. In the Asian Group 2 game, the Iranians scored six times in the first half and 11 in the second, striker Karim Bagheri scoring seven of the 17. The Maldives – who shared Group 2 with Iran, Syria, and Kyrgyzstan – finished with a dismal record of six games played, six losses, zero goals scored, and 59 conceded.

* Shortly before the start of the tournament, the French Chefs' Association protested that it was sponsored by the American hamburger chain McDonald's. 'This alliance between football and fast food is not a gastronomic issue, and one in which a lot of money is at stake. French gastronomy is world-renowned. We can't let a hamburger replace us,' the chefs warned. FIFA dismissed the complaint.

* In the opening match, which pitted Brazil against Scotland at the Stade de France in Saint-Denis on 10 June, South American César Sampaio scored the fastest goal recorded in any World Cup opening match in the fourth minute. Brazil won 2-1.

* On 14 June, at the Stade Félix-Bollaert in Lens, Croatia defeated Jamaica 3-1. One of the European

squad's heroes, Robert Prosinečki, became the first player to score in the World Cup for two different countries: at Italy 1990, Prosinečki had scored against the United Arab Emirates while wearing a Yugoslavia shirt.

* After Saudi Arabia lost their chance of qualifying for the second round of the World Cup, following defeats to Denmark (1-0) and France (4-0), an unprecedented event in World Cup history occurred: the Asian team's Brazilian coach, Carlos Alberto Parreira, was fired before the final match, against South Africa. Barely had the French rout ended on 18 June in Saint-Denis when Prince Faisal bin Fahd Al Saud, son of then-King Fahd bin Abdulaziz and president of the country's football federation, entered the dressing room and dismissed Parreira, who had coached Brazil to victory in the United States four years earlier. Faisal immediately appointed one of the team's technical assistants, Mohamed Al Karashi. With their new tactical coach, Saudi Arabia broke their losing streak against South Africa, and although they drew 2-2, they had been close to a victory: the Africans equalised in the 93rd minute via a penalty.

* During the 1-1 draw between Chile and Cameroon, which closed out Group B on 23 June at the Stade de la Beaujoire in Nantes, Hungarian referee László Vágner showed African defender Rigobert Song a straight red card for elbowing striker Marcelo Salas in the face. Song thus achieved a record having been sent off in two consecutive World Cups. At the 1994 tournament in the United States, Song had been dismissed by Mexican referee Arturo Brizio Carter during Brazil's 3-0 victory over Cameroon.

* That same day yielded two more gems: during Italy's 2-1 victory over Austria at the Stade de France, Giuseppe Bergomi replaced Alessandro Nesta just four minutes after kick-off, the earliest such change in a World Cup match. Meanwhile, at the Stade Vélodrome in Marseille, a young Norwegian man named Oivind Ekeland married his Brazilian girlfriend Rosangela de Souza – just minutes before kick-off of the match between Norway and Brazil. The wedding was approved by FIFA: the organisation's spokesperson, Keith Cooper, stated that the marriage was authorised because 'football should unite people in a spirit of love, friendship, and brotherhood'. Oivind's joy was doubly high, as Norway won 2-1 and secured their place in the round of 16.

* The following day, in Lens, Spain achieved – to that point – their biggest World Cup win, defeating Bulgaria 6-1 in their third game of Group D. However, this comfortable victory was not enough to advance to the second round: after previously losing to Nigeria and drawing with Paraguay they earned four points, two fewer than the Africans (who had also defeated Bulgaria) and one behind the South Americans, who had drawn with the two European teams and defeated the Nigerians in their last match of the opening round.

* On 28 June, in the last 16, France defeated Paraguay in Lens thanks to a rule introduced in this World Cup, which only lasted until the conclusion of the next tournament: the 'golden goal'. If a team scored a goal, the match ended immediately, even if there was still time to play. In France, the only game decided

this way was between the home team and Paraguay. The last-16 tie was settled in the 113th minute when French defender Laurent Blanc collected a headed pass from Zinedine Zidane inside the Paraguayan box and fired a right-footed shot past goalkeeper José Luis Chilavert.

* That same day, in Saint-Denis, Denmark's 4-1 victory over Nigeria set a record that will be difficult to break: in the 58th minute, with the score at 2-0, Ebbe Sand replaced Peter Møller and, just 16 seconds later, scored their third goal, and the quickest goal by a substitute in the history of the World Cup.

* On 30 June, the Stade Geoffroy-Guichard in Saint-Étienne hosted another duel between Argentina and England, the first in the World Cup since Diego Maradona's magical afternoon in Mexico 12 years earlier. After a thrilling first half that ended 2-2, Diego Simeone fouled David Beckham in the first minute of the second period. Beckham responded with a kick from the ground, and Danish referee Kim Milton Nielsen sent him off. With one man fewer, England reined in their attacks, and the match fizzled out without any further goals. In the penalty shoot-out, Argentina prevailed thanks to two saves from their goalkeeper, Carlos Roa. In England, the owner of a Brighton pub filed a lawsuit against Beckham, holding him responsible for the financial losses his business suffered following that defeat.

* Few matches in World Cup history have ended with such a misleading scoreline as the goalless draw between France and Italy in the quarter-finals on 3 July in Saint-Denis. The two teams put on a highly engaging encounter, with dozens of

FRANCE 1998

dangerous chances in front of both goals and brilliant performances from both goalkeepers, Gianluca Pagliuca and Fabien Barthez. In the penalty shoot-out, both men made a save (Barthez from Demetrio Albertini and Pagliuca from Bixente Lizarazu), and the match was only decided when Luigi Di Biagio smashed the crossbar with the final Italian penalty.

* A day later, at the Stade Gerland in Lyon, Croatia stunned Germany by defeating them 3-0. In that match, Germany's Lothar Matthäus, who had already equalled the record of five World Cups played in, held solely by Mexican Antonio Carbajal until France 1998, added another mark: appearing in 25 World Cup matches. Matthäus's record would stand until Qatar 2022, where it would be broken by Argentina's Lionel Messi.

* The semi-final between Brazil and the Netherlands was also decided thanks to a penalty shoot-out. After a 1-1 draw and two thrilling hours, South American goalkeeper Cláudio Taffarel, who also made shoot-out saves in the US four years earlier, once again became a hero, stopping attempts from Phillip Cocu and Ronald de Boer. Brazil won 4-2 and qualified for their second consecutive final.

* In the final, played on 12 July at the Stade de France in Saint-Denis, France annihilated Brazil 3-0 with two goals from Zinedine Zidane and one from Emmanuel Petit, and became world champions for the first time. It had been 20 years since a host team had won the tournament – Argentina in 1978 – and this feat had not been repeated by the time of publication. Two facts highlight France's excellent performance: they won the tournament with the

fewest goals conceded, just two, a circumstance that had not occurred with a winner since 1930; they suffered three red cards throughout the competition – Zidane against Saudi Arabia in the second match of the first round, Laurent Blanc in the semi-final against Croatia and Marcel Desailly in the final against Brazil – which shows that they did not enjoy complicit favouritism on the part of the referees. It could be said, without exaggeration, that France were crowned as absolutely legitimate monarchs.

* 'I felt happier the day France won the World Cup than the day I was elected,' said French president Jacques Chirac, exultant after his country's victory.

* Days after France's success, the Brazilian press revealed that forward Ronaldo had suffered a serious illness hours before the final and had been included in the line-up under pressure from the South American team's sponsorship companies. According to the official version, Ronaldo experienced seizures and, after undergoing numerous tests in a Parisian clinic, coach Mário Zagallo – backed by doctor Lidio Toledo – decided to include him as a starter, despite the first team sheets released not having him in the 11. However, many media outlets claimed that the coach had been forced to introduce Ronaldo by the president of the Brazilian Football Confederation, Ricardo Teixeira. Ronaldo, who performed poorly in the final, confessed years later that his roommate, left-back Roberto Carlos, 'saved my life: we were in the room and I lay down for a nap. I had violent convulsions and lost consciousness for about 30 seconds. I was shaking.' Seeing Ronaldo's state, Roberto Carlos ran to the team doctors, who

immediately treated the striker and managed to revive him.

* Croatian striker Davor Šuker won the Golden Boot for being the top scorer, with six goals. Upon receiving the trophy, Šuker asked for it to be changed because the prize was a boot shaped for the right foot – and he was left-footed!

Statistical focus – players who have scored the most goals in a single World Cup:

Player	Country	Tournament	Goals
Just Fontaine	France	Sweden 1958	13
Sándor Kocsis	Hungary	Switzerland 1954	11
Gerd Müller	Germany	Mexico 1970	10
Eusébio	Portugal	England 1966	9
Guillermo Stábile	Argentina	Uruguay 1930	8
Ademir	Brazil	Brazil 1950	8
Ronaldo	Brazil	S. Korea–Japan 2002	8
Kylian Mbappé	France	Qatar 2022	8

South Korea and Japan 2002

* On 31 May 1996, FIFA's Executive Committee made an unprecedented decision: that the first World Cup of the 21st century would be jointly organised by two nations. South Korea, Japan and Mexico had been bidding to host the 2002 tournament but, with Mexico having already hosted twice previously, it became such a close decision between two Asian countries that FIFA president João Havelange and eight European delegates proposed the first joint World Cup in history, based on 'the excellent work of both candidates and because the thermometer around the world indicated that this was desired'. Havelange indicated that although FIFA's statutes did not allow two countries sharing the competition, they would be modified. 'We decided it was the best solution for the political, sporting, and economic co-existence of the two countries,' he declared. While the union of South Korea and Japan made possible a technologically brilliant World Cup, with 20 stadiums, the largest number in history, the supposedly friendly relationship between the two nations was not revealed as such: resentment between the two peoples from their conflict during the Second World War still lingered. Japanese Emperor Akihito snubbed his partners by not attending the Seoul World Cup Stadium to witness the opening ceremony. Furious, Korean Football Federation president Chung Mong-joon described

SOUTH KOREA AND JAPAN 2002

the snub as 'like a bride or groom not showing up at a wedding'. Despite this discourtesy, the tournament went ahead very smoothly.

* The selection of two Far Eastern countries caused some headaches in the western world. In Argentina and Brazil, fans had to get up very early, or even skip bed, to watch some of the matches, scheduled for 3am. In Europe, many schools and businesses opted to open late on matchdays or installed televisions in common areas so students and employees could watch the games and still meet their obligations.

* The tournament organisers chose the Spheriks as mascots: three indecipherable, futuristic-looking characters who played a football-like sport on an infinite field in the sky. These three creatures are remembered every four years when fans vote for the worst mascot in World Cup history.

* In the South American qualifiers, Colombia, who had participated in the three previous World Cups, were eliminated by a single goal in Uruguay's favour. On the last matchday, Colombia thrashed Paraguay 4-0 away, but a draw between Uruguay and Argentina, who had already qualified several matches earlier, meant *La Celeste* went into a play-off against Australia. Most striking is that, when they faced each other in Bogotá on matchday seven of 18, Colombia won 1-0 but could have increased the score: Uruguayan goalkeeper Fabián Carini saved a penalty from Iván Córdoba. If it had gone in and all other results had stayed the same, the Colombians would have qualified.

* In Asia, the spots secured by hosts South Korea and Japan facilitated the qualification of China, who

secured their only World Cup appearances to date. Three other teams who made their debuts in this edition were Ecuador, Slovenia and Senegal.

* In Oceania, Australia scored 53 goals in two days: on 9 April 2001 they crushed Tonga 22-0, and 48 hours later they humiliated American Samoa 31-0. This scoreline remains the highest in World Cup history. Australian striker Archie Thompson also became the all-time top scorer in a single qualifying match, with 13 goals. In the first round, Australia scored 66 goals against Fiji, Tonga, Samoa, and American Samoa, and conceded none. Then, in the play-off, they beat New Zealand 6-1 on aggregate. However, despite their scoring prowess at home, Australia still failed to qualify, losing the intercontinental play-off to Uruguay. They won 1-0 in Melbourne but lost 3-0 at Montevideo's legendary Estadio Centenario.

* For this tournament, FIFA made some technical innovations, such as increasing the number of players per squad to 23, and stipulating that the champions would no longer qualify directly for the following World Cup.

* In 2002, France, the last winners to automatically go to the next tournament to defend their title, produced the worst performance ever for a champion in the following World Cup: they lost 1-0 to Senegal, drew 0-0 with Uruguay, and fell 2-0 to Denmark, bowing out in the first round without scoring a single goal.

* China's debut was very poor: they lost to Costa Rica, Brazil, and Turkey, and didn't score a goal either. Their coach, Bora Milutinović, revealed in an interview a few years later that, shortly before the start of the tournament, he had entered a church

to pray for his team to have a good performance. 'God asked me, "What do you want, Bora?" And I said, "To achieve the same as France."' And so it was: in Korea and Japan, France and China were the only two teams who failed to score, and both were eliminated in the first round. 'I was aiming,' the Serb lamented, 'to achieve what France had done in 1998.'

* On 1 June at Japan's Sapporo Dome, Germany achieved their most resounding victory in the World Cup, crushing Saudi Arabia 8-0. Three of their goals were scored by Miroslav Klose, who thus began his path to becoming the all-time top scorer in World Cup history.

* On 4 June at the Asiad Arena in Busan, South Korea secured their first victory in six World Cup appearances, 2-0 against Poland thanks to goals from Hwang Sun-hong and Yoo Sang-chul. Defender Cha Du-ri was booked just 20 seconds after coming on to the field. Cha replaced Seol Hi-kyeon in the 89th minute, and was quickly cautioned by Colombian referee Óscar Ruiz for a foul on Polish goalkeeper Jerzy Dudek.

* A day later, at the World Cup Stadium in Suwon, the USA's Jeff Agoos and Portugal's Jorge Costa both scored an own goal in the same World Cup match. The Americans triumphed 3-2, a victory that ultimately allowed them to advance to the next round and, at the same time, send the Portuguese home.

* David Beckham got sweet revenge on 7 June when England beat Argentina 1-0 in Sapporo: he scored the only goal of the match, a penalty. Beckham not only managed to erase the bitter taste of his red card in England's last-16 defeat to Argentina four years

earlier, but his team's victory would also allow them to qualify a few days later – after a draw against Nigeria – and Argentina to be eliminated, which happened after their draw with Sweden.

* Germany v Cameroon on 11 June in Shizuoka was a very tough match: Spanish referee Antonio López Nieto had to caution 14 players, seven from each team. Two of them received two yellow cards, resulting in their dismissals: Germany's Carsten Ramelow and Cameroon's Patrick Suffo, who had come on as a substitute in the 53rd minute, replacing Bill Tchato, and was on the pitch for just 24 minutes.

* Argentina were eliminated in the first round for the first time since Chile in 1962. Marcelo Bielsa's squad began the competition with a victory over Nigeria, but a defeat to England and a draw with Sweden left them in third place in the table, behind the two European sides. On the day of the draw against Sweden, on 12 June at Miyagi Stadium in Rifu, an incredible event occurred: forward Claudio Caniggia received a red card without having played a single second of the match. In the 47th minute, Caniggia, sitting on the substitutes' bench, insulted referee Ali Bujsaim of the United Arab Emirates. The official didn't understand the insult, but one of his assistants, Jamaican Peter Prendergast, who spoke some Spanish and was standing a few metres away, did. Prendergast informed Bujsaim of the situation, and he approached the bench and sent off Caniggia.

* Japan, who had debuted four years earlier in France with three losses, not only qualified for the second round, but also finished first in their group,

something never before achieved by an Asian team. They had started with a 2-2 draw against Belgium. They then defeated Russia 1-0 and Tunisia 2-0, the latter game on 14 June. That same day, a few hours later, South Korea also secured a place in the second round, also in first place.

* On 17 June, in the Korean city of Jeonju, an exceptional match between Mexico and the United States took place. This remains their only World Cup meeting in more than 80 official matches. It aroused such anticipation in both countries that, the day before the game, US president George Bush called his Mexican counterpart Vicente Fox to wish him luck. According to reports published by several newspapers, Bush also spoke with his team's coach, Bruce Arena. 'The country is very proud of you. Many people who know nothing about soccer, like me, are very excited and are rooting for you,' he expressed. The message lifted the spirits of the American team, who won 2-0, thanks to goals from Brian McBride and Landon Donovan, and for the only time in their history won a match in the second round of the World Cup.

* As is often the case at the World Cup, some refereeing decisions have proven controversial. On 17 June, in the Japanese city of Kobe, Jamaican referee Peter Prendergast disallowed a legitimate goal by Belgian striker Marc Wilmots against Brazil when the score was still 0-0. The South Americans then won 2-0 thanks to the power of their magnificent stars including Ronaldinho, Ronaldo, Rivaldo (all three Ballon d'Or winners), Roberto Carlos, and Cafu, among others.

* The following day, another scandal erupted when Italy – who also had a superb team coached by Giovanni Trapattoni and comprised, among other stars, Gianluigi Buffon, Paolo Maldini, Alessandro Del Piero, Christian Vieri, and Francesco Totti – lost to a feisty South Korea in extra time of their last-16 match played on 18 June in Daejeon. Several European media outlets condemned the performance of Ecuadorian referee Byron Moreno, accusing him of unfairly sending off Totti for a second yellow card and of disallowing a Damiano Tomassi goal for offside, even though, according to reports, he was in the right position. That goal, scored during extra time, would have meant a 'golden goal' for the *Azzurri*. Three minutes from the end of extra time, Ahn Jung-hwan scored a goal that did indeed prove to be 'golden', sealing a 2-1 victory for Korea. RAI, the state-run television network that broadcast Italy's matches, announced it would sue FIFA for damages.

* On 21 June, the electrifying quarter-final between Brazil and England had the feel of an early final. England opened the scoring when the fiery Michael Owen capitalised on a mistake by defender Lúcio to beat goalkeeper Marcos with a masterful touch. But Brazil, brimming with genius, rubbed the lamp: first Rivaldo equalised with a lethal left-footed shot as the first half ended, then a Ronaldinho free kick surprised veteran goalkeeper David Seaman and found the net in the top-right corner in the 50th minute. Shortly afterwards, Brazil lost Ronaldinho, sent off for a tackle on England's Danny Mills. However, they maintained their lead and advanced to the next round.

* The controversies didn't end in the last 16. In the next stage, South Korea defeated Spain on penalties on 22 June in Gwangju. However, the result was harshly criticised by Spanish footballers and fans – and by the European and South American press. 'Assault with a raised flag' headlined the Catalan newspaper *El Mundo Deportivo*, which blamed the two linesmen for the defeat – Trinidadian Michael Ragoonath and Ugandan Ali Tomusange; Ragoonath for wrongly indicating that the ball had crossed the line after a pass from Joaquín Sánchez Rodríguez, which Fernando Morientes headed into the net, and Tomusange for indicating that Luis Enrique was in a non-existent offside position when he was running all alone towards the goal defended by goalkeeper Lee Woon-jae. To make matters worse, that action was in extra time, with the possibility of Spain winning with a 'golden goal'. Egyptian referee Gamal Ahmed Al-Ghandour also made an important error: he disallowed an own goal by home defender Kim Tae-young, for an alleged foul after he headed a Spanish cross into Woon-jae's net. The footage clearly showed that no Spaniard had pushed or made illegal contact with Tae-young.

* 'The mistakes of my assistants shouldn't count against me,' said Gamal Ahmed Al-Ghandour, interviewed by the Spanish newspaper *Marca* 20 years after the controversial match.

* Also on 22 June, Turkey, who had eliminated Japan in the quarter-finals, narrowly defeated Senegal and advanced to the semi-finals. They won 1-0 thanks to a goal by İlhan Mansız, a young man who was born in Germany and had become a Turkish citizen. The

only goal came in extra time, so the match ended as soon as the ball touched the net. Mansız scored the fourth and final 'golden goal' in World Cup history, as FIFA abolished this rule before the start of the next tournament.

* South Korea's good run was cut short against Germany on 25 June in Seoul. The home side struggled against a well-organised defence and the confident hands of Oliver Kahn, who had conceded just one goal in the opening round and kept clean sheets in the last 16 against Paraguay and the quarter-final against the United States. The Germans won with a single goal from Michael Ballack and qualified for the final. South Korea took the consolation of being the only Asian team to reach a semi-final in the entire history of the World Cup.

* The following day, in the Japanese city of Saitama, Brazil eliminated Turkey, also 1-0, with a strike from Ronaldo, who added his sixth goal of the tournament. Brazil were the far superior team despite missing the suspended Ronaldinho.

* Third-place matches usually garner little interest. However, Turkey's victory over South Korea set an incredible record in World Cup history: Turkish captain Hakan Şükür scored a goal with just 10.8 seconds gone in an eventual 3-2 win. The brave Korean players were left without a medal, but they were still rewarded: the government ruled that all 23 members of the squad would be exempt from compulsory military service. Dutch coach Guus Hiddink, meanwhile, was rewarded by a Seoul hotel, the Westin Chosun, with free beer for life.

SOUTH KOREA AND JAPAN 2002

* The final, held at Yokohama International Stadium on 30 June, pitted the two teams with the most World Cup appearances against each other in the tournament for the first time: Brazil and Germany. The quality of the South Americans, with Ronaldinho back on the pitch after serving a one-match suspension, proved too much for the efficient Germans. Rudi Völler, who as a player had been a World Cup winner in 1990, was left wanting to join the select club of those who have won the competition as both players and coaches. After a goalless first half, in which the crossbar and Oliver Kahn kept the Germany goal intact, two extraordinary actions by Ronaldo – in both cases with the invaluable collaboration of Rivaldo – defined the final: for the first goal, *O Fenômeno* took advantage of Kahn's letting slip a shot; for the second, Ronaldo capitalised on a feint by his colleague, which unsettled the entire German defence, and drove the ball just inside the post, well beyond Kahn's reach. Brazil more than justified their fifth World Cup after winning all seven matches played.

* 'When I score goals, I'm big; if not, I'm fat,' said Ronaldo, top scorer in 2002 with eight goals.

Statistical focus – biggest World Cup wins:

Match	*Tournament*
Hungary 10 El Salvador 1	Spain 1982
Hungary 9 South Korea 0	Switzerland 1954
Yugoslavia 9 Zaire 0	Germany 1974
Sweden 8 Cuba 0	France 1938
Uruguay 8 Bolivia 0	Brazil 1950
Germany 8 Saudi Arabia 0	South Korea and Japan 2002

Germany 2006

* Germany's selection as the 2006 host nation unleashed a long and intense chain of complaints. Several newspapers, including *The Guardian* in England, reported that the president of the Oceania Football Federation, Charles Dempsey, a naturalised New Zealander from Scotland, had received $250,000 to favour the selection of Germany over South Africa, the other country bidding to host the greatest sporting tournament in human history. According to the newspaper, Dempsey, who had publicly stated that he would vote for the African nation, abstained from the final vote after receiving the bribe, allowing Germany to win 12 to 11 in the election held in Zurich on 7 July 2000. The African continent had to wait four more years to finally secure the World Cup hosting rights.

* The qualifying stage produced several surprises. Trinidad and Tobago, a small Caribbean island nation of just 5,000 square kilometres (under 2,000 square miles), reached Germany after finishing fourth in the CONCACAF final round and defeating Bahrain in the intercontinental play-off against Asian representatives. The Trinidadians represented the smallest country to participate in the World Cup finals in the competition's history.

* In the African group, four of the five qualified teams reached the World Cup for the first time: Angola,

Ghana, Togo, and Ivory Coast. Angola impressed in their group, beating experienced World Cup teams such as Nigeria and Algeria; Togo defeated Senegal, who had performed quite successfully in South Korea and Japan 2002; Ghana easily prevailed ahead of, among others, South Africa; Ivory Coast probably caused the biggest surprise, outperforming powerful teams such as Egypt and Cameroon. Tunisia, who had already participated in the World Cups in 1978, 1998 and 2002, finished fifth.

* The qualifying round proved unhappy for Cameroon's Pierre Womé. On 7 October 2005, in the final match of African Group 3, a victory at the Stade Omnisports Ahmadou Ahidjo in Yaoundé against eliminated Egypt would have secured their qualification ahead of Ivory Coast. In the 95th minute, with the score at 1-1, Malian referee Koman Coulibaly awarded a penalty for the home side. The crucial shot, the final action of the match, was taken by Womé, who unleashed a powerful left-footed drive: the ball hit the base of goalkeeper Essam el Hadary's post and bounced out. Fans, furious that their national team had been eliminated from the World Cup, attempted to lynch their players. Womé, an Inter Milan defender, had to be taken from the stadium to the airport without even showering, to catch a plane to Europe before a mob could gorge itself on his blood. The rabid fans retaliated by destroying Womé's house and his Mercedes-Benz car.

* In Europe, the qualifications of the Czech Republic and Serbia and Montenegro, two states with World Cup history – albeit in conjunction with other nations – were not particularly noteworthy. The Czechs

had formed Czechoslovakia with Slovakia, and the Serbo-Montenegrins had formed the old Yugoslavia, a collection of countries brought together by the political upheavals of the 20th century, primarily as a result of the First World War. On the Old Continent, Ukraine also qualified for the first time, having not only been a previous part of the former Soviet Union but also nurturing the socialist conglomerate's team with many stars.

* The opening match of the tournament did not feature the previous edition's champions, Brazil. This custom, which had been in place since West Germany in 1974, was changed after FIFA decided that the World Cup winners would not automatically qualify for the next competition. Host Germany defeated Costa Rica 4-2 in Munich.

* On 10 June in Frankfurt, England started with a victory over Paraguay. The only goal of the match was not scored by an England player, but by Paraguayan defender Carlos Gamarra: after David Beckham launched a cross from the left, Gamarra jumped and tried to keep the ball out, but it ended up in the net of Justo Villar's goal. The South American's ill-fated goal went down in history as the fastest own goal in World Cup history, just three minutes into the first half.

* Mexico's debut had a very special flavour, and not just because of the victory over Iran on 11 June in Nuremberg. Starting goalkeeper Oswaldo Sánchez played virtually without sleep because he had to return to Mexico to attend his father's funeral. After learning of his death, Sánchez travelled urgently to Guadalajara, went to the funeral, and returned

to Germany to rejoin his team-mates. Sánchez arrived at the hotel where the squad was staying in Göttingen the night before the opening match against Iran. Coach Ricardo la Volpe included him in the team that won 3-1, and Sánchez, who put in a superb performance, broke down at the final whistle: he knelt and mourned his father. In the stands of the stadium, Oswaldo's mother, Alma Rosa, watched the match hugging the vase that held the ashes of her late husband and proud father of Oswaldo.

* In Group A, Ecuador's 3-0 victory over Costa Rica on 15 June in Hamburg, which qualified the South American team for the second round for the first time, featured a special celebration: forward Iván Kaviedes, who scored the third goal, celebrated his triumph by donning a yellow mask similar to the one worn by Spider-Man in comics or movies. Neither the referee nor FIFA sanctioned Kaviedes: his gesture was intended to honour Otilino Tenorio, a former team-mate of his with the national team and Emelec, who had died a few months before the World Cup in a car accident. Tenorio, who died at the age of 25 and had participated in several matches in the qualifying round, had a custom of celebrating his goals by donning a Spider-Man mask.

* A day later, in Gelsenkirchen, Argentina crushed Serbia and Montenegro 6-0. The rout was notable because two years earlier, at the 2004 Athens Olympics, the South Americans had also defeated the same opponents by the same scoreline. Furthermore, six Argentine players were present in both sweeping victories: Roberto Ayala, Gabriel Heinze, Javier Mascherano, Carlos Tevez, Luis González and Javier

Saviola. Tevez was the only player to score in both matches: two goals in the Olympics and one in the World Cup.

* Argentina's sweeping victory over Serbia and Montenegro yielded a gem: Lionel Messi made his World Cup debut, and he also scored his first goal in the competition. Over the years and World Cups, *La Pulga* (The Flea, in Spanish) would become the player with the most matches (26) and minutes (2,316) played across Germany 2006, South Africa 2010, Brazil 2014, Russia 2018, and Qatar 2022.

* A few hours later, during the match between Portugal and Iran in Frankfurt on 17 June, Cristiano Ronaldo scored his first World Cup goal. This success opened an unparalleled streak, as he is the only player to have scored in five World Cups. The forward did it in Germany 2006, South Africa 2010, Brazil 2014, Russia 2018 and Qatar 2022.

* On 22 June in Stuttgart, English referee Graham Poll showed the same player three yellow cards. The unusual situation occurred during the crucial Group F match between Croatia and Australia. A win for either side would have seen them qualify, while a draw favoured the Australians. Defender Josip Šimunić – who, coincidentally, was born in Australia but had acquired Croatian nationality – was booked in the 61st minute, with the score at 2-1 in favour of the Europeans, and again in the 90th minute, when the game was level at 2-2. Despite the second yellow card, Šimunić remained on the field, as neither the referee, his assistants, nor the Australians noticed the irregularity. In extra time, in the 93rd minute, Šimunić exaggeratedly protested Poll's decision and

was booked again. The third time was the charm, and the new yellow card was accompanied by a red. Australia held on to a draw until the end and became the first team from Oceania to qualify for the second round of the World Cup.

* Tunisian captain Riadh Bouazizi experienced a rather unusual situation: he was substituted in each of his team's Group H matches: against Saudi Arabia, he was replaced by Mehdi Nafti in the 55th minute; against Spain, Alaeddine Yahia in the 57th; against Ukraine, Chaouki Ben Saada in the 79th. Tunisia drew 2-2 with Saudi Arabia and lost the other two, 3-1 and 1-0, respectively.

* The duel between Portugal and the Netherlands on 25 June in the last 16 was so violent that it was described by the press as the 'Battle of Nuremberg'. The kicking fest caused, for example, Portuguese forward Cristiano Ronaldo to leave the game in the 33rd minute after receiving a blow to his right thigh from Khalid Boulahrouz, which clearly deserved a red card. Ronaldo left the field with tears in his eyes. A few seconds before the end of the first half – with the score 1-0 to Portugal, scored by Nuno Maniche – Russian referee Valentin Ivanov sent off Portuguese forward Francisco Costinha for a second yellow card: one for fouling Phillip Cocu; the other for handling the ball in a midfield play that did not pose a risk to his goal. In the second half, the number of beatings increased. After Giovanni van Bronckhorst brought down Deco, Luís Figo head-butted Mark van Bommel in the face. The referee, who didn't see the attack because he had his back turned, booked Van Bronckhorst, and only showed a yellow card to the

Portuguese captain, who deserved the red for having hit his rival. Ivanov then sent off Boulahrouz, van Bronckhorst and Deco, all for second bookings, although Deco should have been sent off directly for making a tackle from behind against John Heitinga. In total, the referee issued 16 yellow cards and four reds, a record for a World Cup match.

* 'Jesus Christ may be able to turn the other cheek, but Luís Figo is not Jesus Christ,' said Portugal coach Luiz Felipe Scolari during the press conference after his team's brutal match against the Netherlands.

* On 26 June in Cologne, Switzerland reached a rare milestone: they were eliminated without losing – or conceding a single goal throughout the entire competition. Their curious performance began in Group G with a goalless draw against France and two 2-0 wins against Togo and South Korea. In the next round, Switzerland faced Ukraine in a lacklustre match that ended in a goalless draw after two hours of play. In the penalty shoot-out, the Swiss players missed three times which led to a 3-0 victory for Ukraine.

* With his goal against Ghana on 27 June in Dortmund in the round of 16, Brazilian striker Ronaldo surpassed German marksman Gerd Müller as the all-time leading scorer in World Cup history. Ronaldo, who had already scored four goals in France 1998 and eight in South Korea–Japan 2002, added two against Japan in the group phase and another against Ghana, giving him 15 goals and surpassing Müller by one. Brazil had also won 11 consecutive World Cup games, a feat never equalled or surpassed in the history of the tournament. They won all their matches in South

Korea–Japan 2002 and had now defeated Croatia, Australia, Japan, and Ghana in Germany.

* In the quarter-finals, Germany defeated Argentina after a penalty shoot-out. The match, played on 30 June at the Olympic Stadium in Berlin, had ended 1-1 after two hours of play. German goalkeeper Jens Lehmann saved from Roberto Ayala and Esteban Cambiasso, which gave the home team the victory, thanks to information a staff member had written on a piece of paper about the South Americans' shots in penalty shoot-outs or similar situations. During the shoot-out, Lehmann hid the sheet of paper in one of his socks and took it out before each attempt to study his opponents. After qualifying for the semi-finals, the goalkeeper donated the sheet to the Museum of Contemporary History in Bonn, where it was added to an art exhibition.

* On 1 July in Gelsenkirchen, Portugal also defeated England in a penalty shoot-out, after 90 minutes and extra time ended goalless. The 3-1 success was made possible by Ricardo Pereira's three saves – from Frank Lampard, Steven Gerrard, and Jamie Carragher – a feat no goalkeeper had achieved up to that point in the World Cup.

* France, led by the brilliant Zinedine Zidane, ended Brazil's winning streak in the quarter-finals, winning 1-0 thanks to a goal from Thierry Henry. Then, in the semi-finals, they also halted the triumphant march of Luiz Felipe Scolari, who had coached Brazil in 2002 and in charge of Portugal had four wins in Germany and a draw with a shoot-out victory. *Felipão*'s unbeaten run ended with a single goal from Zidane, a penalty.

* The 2006 World Cup Final, played between Italy and France on 9 July at the Olympic Stadium in Berlin, featured a notable number of Juventus players: Italy's Gianluigi Buffon, Mauro Camoranesi, Fabio Cannavaro, Gianluca Zambrotta, and Alessandro Del Piero, and Frenchmen Lilian Thuram, David Trezeguet, and Patrick Vieira. Among the finalists were players who had also worn the *Bianconeri* jersey in previous seasons: Italians Fabio Grosso, Andrea Pirlo, Simone Perrotta, Luca Toni, and Vincenzo Iaquinta, and France's Zinedine Zidane and Thierry Henry.

* With the score tied at 1-1 the respective scorers, Marco Materazzi and Zinedine Zidane, engaged in a heated argument that culminated in an unusual assault: the French captain head-butted his opponent on the chest, who fell to the turf as if hit by shrapnel. Argentine referee Horacio Elizondo – the first to officiate the opening match and the final of the same World Cup – didn't see the assault, but sent Zidane off after being informed by the fourth official, Spaniard Luis Medina Cantalejo. After the match, Zidane admitted to having made 'an unforgivable gesture', although he emphasised that Materazzi had uttered 'very harsh, very serious words that touched me deeply. I would have preferred a punch in the face to hearing that.' The final ended without any further goals, and Italy were crowned champions after winning the penalty shoot-out 5-3. David Trezeguet produced the only miss: his shot bounced off the crossbar.

* Zinedine Zidane is the most penalised player in World Cup history: he received four yellow cards

and two reds in 12 World Cup matches, from France 1998 to Germany 2006. This tournament, meanwhile, remained the one with the most cards, with 28 reds and 345 yellows, since Mexico 1970, when this penalty system began to be used.

* 'When a player wins the World Cup, he becomes a legend,' said victorious Italy captain Fabio Cannavaro.

Statistical focus – coaches with the most World Cup appearances:

Coach	World Cups	Countries
Carlos Alberto Parreira	6	Kuwait (1982), United Arab Emirates (1990), Brazil (1994, 2006), Saudi Arabia (1998), South Africa (2010)
Bora Milutinović	5	Mexico (1986), Costa Rica (1990), USA (1994), Nigeria (1998), China (2002)
Sepp Herberger	4	Germany (1938, 1954, 1958, 1962)
Walter Winterbottom	4	England (1950, 1954, 1958, 1962)
Lajos Baróti	4	Hungary (1958, 1962, 1966, 1978)
Helmut Schön	4	Germany (1966, 1970, 1974, 1978)
Henri Michel	4	France (1986), Cameroon (1994), Morocco (1998), Ivory Coast (2006)
Óscar Tabárez	4	Uruguay (1990, 2010, 2014, 2018)

SOUTH AFRICA 2010

* The 2010 World Cup was predestined. Nine years earlier, the then-FIFA president Sepp Blatter had declared that the tournament would be played in Africa. Therefore, at the organisation's Congress held in Zurich on 15 May 2001, only nations from that continent submitted bids: Egypt, Morocco, Libya, and South Africa. In the vote, South Africa defeated Morocco 14 to 10 (remarkably, the winner was supported by the American delegates, the loser by the Africans) and was awarded the hosting rights.

* African motifs were prominent in the organisation of and throughout the tournament. Adidas decorated the official ball with 11 colours, representing the number of players on a football team, but also the 11 communities and 11 official languages (including English) of South Africa. The ball was named Jabulani, which in Zulu, the most commonly spoken language in the country, means 'to celebrate'. The World Cup mascot, meanwhile, was Zakumi, a leopard with green hair. Its name came from the conjunction of the acronym ZA, which represents South Africa in several international languages, and the expression *kumi*, which in Zulu and other regional languages means 'ten'. The World Cup also had a resounding character that made its presence felt: the vuvuzela. This musical wind instrument typical of the southern half of Africa filled the stadiums with its deafening sound. Many players and coaches

complained about the powerful roar caused by the shrill trumpet, comparable to the buzzing of a swarm of millions of bees. Throughout the tournament, sales of earplugs skyrocketed, driven by demand from visiting fans: one Cape Town merchant claimed to have sold out in two days, even though the plugs barely reduced the sound from 120 to 90 decibels. Television networks broadcasting the matches reduced the ambient noise from the stadiums, but did not eliminate it entirely, so as not to make them seem empty, so that the vuvuzelas would not drown out the voices of their commentators. After the World Cup, the football associations of all American and European countries banned their use in stadiums.

* The European qualifiers allowed two debuting nations to participate: Slovakia, which had been part of Czechoslovakia, and Serbia, which had been included in the former Yugoslavia. Meanwhile, France's qualification, after they finished second in their group behind Serbia, proved highly controversial. They won 1-0 in Dublin in the first leg of their play-off against the Republic of Ireland. In the second leg, played at the Stade de France, the Irish took the lead on the night thanks to an exquisite finish from Robbie Keane that levelled the tie. Thirteen minutes into extra time, William Gallas scored after receiving a pass from Thierry Henry. But the goal should have been disallowed because, in the build-up, Henry had knocked down a Florent Malouda free kick with his hand.

* Italy's path to South Africa was aided immensely by a huge helping hand: on 5 September 2009 at the Boris Paichadze Coliseum in Tbilisi, the *Azzurri*

defeated Georgia 2-0. The curious thing about this match is that both goals were own goals scored by Georgian defender Kakha Kaladze, who at the time was playing for an Italian club, AC Milan. What's more, Kaladze played that day against two of his *Rossoneri* team-mates, Andrea Pirlo and Gianluca Zambrotta. The home fans took the blunder with humour as Georgia had already been eliminated.

* Meanwhile, Africa achieved its largest presence in World Cup history, with six teams. In addition to the host nation, five teams reached the finals: Cameroon, Algeria, Ghana, Nigeria, and Ivory Coast.

* Asia had four representatives: Australia – in their first participation in the Asian Football Confederation, which it had joined a few years earlier – Japan, and both Koreas, South and North. Bahrain could have joined their continental colleagues, but lost in the play-off to New Zealand. Thus, Oceania had two nations in South Africa, although one of them represented a different federation.

* In South America, Argentina secured qualification thanks to former hero Diego Maradona, who had taken over as national coach with just eight matches remaining in qualifying. They confirmed their place on the final day, defeating Uruguay at the Estadio Centenario, finishing behind Brazil, Paraguay, and Chile. The Uruguayan team also secured their spot, albeit after winning a play-off against Costa Rica.

* Two of the stadiums – Mbombela in Nelspruit and Peter Mokaba in Polokwane – featured a new surface combining grass and synthetic carpet. Thus, for the first time in the World Cup, some matches were played on surfaces that were not 100 per cent natural.

SOUTH AFRICA 2010

* In Group A, South Africa drew 1-1 with Mexico in the opening match, then lost 3-0 to Uruguay, and beat France 2-1. The victory was not enough to finish ahead of Mexico and Uruguay, who advanced to the next round. South Africa became the first World Cup host team to be eliminated in the group stage.

* Sixty years after the first meeting between England and the United States, at the 1950 World Cup in Brazil, these two teams faced off again on 12 June at the Royal Bafokeng Stadium in Rustenburg, in Group C. England couldn't avenge their surprise 1-0 defeat in Belo Horizonte, but at least the 1-1 draw helped them to reach the second round – alongside their American cousins.

* When Serbia and Ghana faced each other on 13 June at Loftus Versfeld Field in Pretoria, Balkan native Dejan Stanković achieved a unique record: wearing the shirts of three different countries in three World Cups. Stanković played for Yugoslavia in France 1998, for Serbia and Montenegro in Germany 2006, and for Serbia in South Africa 2010. This peculiarity was due to the various political changes that took place in the Balkans following the disintegration of the former Yugoslavia, beginning with the civil war of 1991.

* On 21 June, at the Green Point Coliseum in Cape Town, Portugal achieved their largest World Cup victory, crushing North Korea 7-0. An interesting fact about this triumph was that the goals were scored by six different players: Raúl Meireles, Simão Sabrosa, Hugo Almeida, Liédson, Cristiano Ronaldo, and Tiago Mendes, the only one with two.

* An unusual event occurred when Ghana and Germany met at Soccer City Stadium in Johannesburg in Group D on 23 June: for the first time in the World Cup, two brothers, Kevin-Prince Boateng and Jérôme Boateng, faced each other wearing the shirts of different countries. In fact, the Boatengs, who were born in Berlin, were half-brothers, as they shared a father but not a mother. In Johannesburg, Jérôme celebrated Germany's 1-0 victory, although the two boys ended up hugging each other and happy because both teams had qualified for the next round.

* In Group E, Japan secured their second qualification for the last 16, their first away from home. They defeated Cameroon 1-0 and Denmark 3-1, finishing second in their group, after a 1-0 fall to the Netherlands.

* Italy were unable to repeat their triumph of four years earlier and were eliminated from their group after drawing with Paraguay and New Zealand. They also suffered a surprising defeat against Slovakia, who had never won a World Cup game and were making their debut in the tournament under that political name. Until the 1994 tournament in the United States, Slovakian players had been part of the Czechoslovakia squad, along with their Czech neighbours. On 24 June at Ellis Park Stadium in Johannesburg, Slovakia won 3-2, securing a place in the next round and also having the pleasure of eliminating the defending champions. As France also failed to make it out of Group A, for the first time, the previous edition's winners and runners-up were eliminated at the initial stage. Coaches Raymond Domenech and Marcello Lippi were

quickly dismissed, and both teams returned to their homeland amid the rejection and insults of the fans.

* Spain, meanwhile, got off to a poor start: on 12 June they lost 1-0 to Switzerland at the Moses Mabhida Coliseum in Durban. However, they qualified for the next round after defeating Honduras 2-0 and Chile 2-1, but also thanks to the Hondurans' 0-0 draw with the Swiss. Switzerland were eliminated but they set a record for minutes without conceding a goal in a World Cup, reaching 559. The run began on 2 July 1994, in the last 16 in the United States, when they were eliminated – coincidentally – by Spain. Switzerland returned to the tournament in Germany 2006, where they drew 0-0 with France, beat Togo and South Korea 2-0, and drew 0-0 with Ukraine in the last 16 after 120 minutes before losing a penalty shoot-out. In South Africa they beat Spain 1-0 in their first match and lost 1-0 to Chile in their second, with a 75th-minute goal by Mark González ending the streak. Another rarity is that the record was achieved by three different goalkeepers: Marco Pascolo in 1994, Pascal Zuberbühler in 2006, and Diego Benaglio in 2010.

* All referees have made and will make mistakes during a match. None was more exposed than Italy's Roberto Rosetti, who was in charge on 27 June when Mexico met Argentina at Soccer City Stadium in Johannesburg in the last 16. In the 26th minute, Argentine magician Lionel Messi left Carlos Tevez facing the goal. Goalkeeper Óscar Pérez's quick exit cut off that advance at the penalty spot, but the ball returned to Messi, who immediately launched a high, deep pass that Tevez headed into the net.

Linesman Paolo Calcagno, somewhat hesitantly, walked to the middle of the field, signalling that, from his perspective, the goal had been valid. After consulting his team-mate via intercom, Rosetti extended his right index finger toward the centre circle. While the Argentine players celebrated the opening goal, the Mexicans pounced on Calcagno, demanding that he inform Rosetti that Tevez had scored in a clear offside position. Rosetti approached the group, and while they argued, the stadium's giant screens replayed the controversial incident. The referee, players from both teams, the two benches, and the 84,000 fans packed into the stands were able to corroborate that the goalscorer had indeed headed the ball from an illegal position. There was no doubt about it. But the rules didn't allow the referee to rely on external factors to review a decision, so Rosetti had to uphold a goal that made him complicit in an injustice. Argentina took advantage of Mexico's nerves and lack of concentration, scoring twice more and advancing to the quarter-finals.

* That same day, at the Free State Stadium in Bloemfontein, Germany and England faced each other. In the 39th minute, with the score 2-1 to the Germans, England midfielder Frank Lampard fired a shot from outside the Germany penalty area that beat goalkeeper Manuel Neuer, hit the crossbar, and bounced about 60 centimetres behind the goal line. But the ball then bounced back out and was immediately taken by Neuer. Neither Uruguayan referee Jorge Larrionda nor his assistant referee and compatriot Emanuel Espinosa recognised that Lampard had scored a legitimate goal, and they ordered play to continue, despite the protests of the

English players. Perhaps discouraged, England were ultimately humiliated 4-1 by their opponents.

* The two refereeing errors that harmed Mexico and England forced FIFA to take action. President Sepp Blatter apologised to both teams and announced that technological elements such as television cameras would be incorporated to prevent these types of unjustifiable incidents. 'We need to discuss again the inclusion of the Hawk-Eye [a camera placed to determine whether a ball crosses the goal line or not]. Personally, I regret it when obvious refereeing errors are seen, but this is not the end of the competition or the end of football; these things can happen,' commented Blatter, who a few months later would be dismissed and suspended for his alleged involvement in corruption cases.

* Uruguay and Ghana were the protagonists of one of the most thrilling matches, with an incredible ending, in almost 100 years of World Cup history. After the first 90 minutes ended 1-1, extra time progressed with many scoring opportunities. With just ten seconds left Ghana's John Pantsil launched a cross into the Uruguayan box. After numerous attempts and deflections, the ball floated to the head of Dominic Adiyiah, who sent it towards the goal. But on its way the ball was deflected by the hands of striker Luis Suárez. Penalty, and Suárez was sent off! Asamoah Gyan took charge but his shot hit the crossbar and went out. Uruguay miraculously survived. In the penalty shoot-out, goalkeeper Fernando Muslera saved shots from John Mensah and the hapless Adiyiah, and Uruguay advanced after a masterful Panenka-style effort from Sebastián

Abreu, feinting a powerful shot and gently lifting the ball into the net. Suárez, a spectator from the tunnel, celebrated the goal as if he himself had scored.

* 'The real Hand of God is mine. I made the best save of the tournament. Sometimes in training I play goalkeeper, so it was worth it,' said Luis Suárez of his controversial handball against Ghana.

* The following day, Germany crushed Diego Maradona's Argentina 4-0, and Spain and Paraguay faced another heart-stopping box-to-box game. In the 57th minute, Guatemalan referee Carlos Batres awarded a penalty to Paraguay for Gerard Piqué's foul on Oscar Cardozo inside the box. Cardozo himself unleashed a powerful left-footed shot which was saved by Iker Casillas. Three minutes later, Batres awarded another penalty, this time for Spain, after Antolín Alcaraz fouled David Villa inside the area. Xabi Alonso took the ball but his right-footed shot was blocked by goalkeeper Justo Villar. The intense match was decided in the 83rd minute when Villa's shot bounced off both posts and found the net.

* With the semi-finals over, with victories for Spain (1-0 against Germany) and the Netherlands (3-2 against Uruguay), the Spaniards had the chance to lift their first World Cup and, at the same time, become the first European team to win outside their continent. A single goal from Andrés Iniesta in the 116th minute broke the deadlock in a match that had several violent passages: English referee Howard Webb showed 14 yellow cards alongside a red for Dutchman John Heitinga, a record for a final. In truth, Webb should have given one fewer caution and one more dismissal: in the 28th minute, the

fiery midfielder Nigel de Jong kicked Xabi Alonso in the chest, which should have been punished with a direct red card. Spain were also the winners with the fewest goals scored, eight, and the first team to win the World Cup after opening with a defeat, against Switzerland, in the group stage.

* For the first time, the Golden Ball award for best player of the tournament went to a footballer whose team didn't make the podium: Diego Forlán. The Uruguayan striker was the driving force and top scorer, with five goals, of a courageous team that finished fourth – behind Spain, the Netherlands, and Germany.

* 'Success without honour is the greatest failure,' said Vicente del Bosque, Spain's World Cup-winning coach.

* The tournament had four top scorers: Germany's Thomas Müller, Spain's David Villa, the Netherlands' Wesley Sneijder, and Uruguay's Diego Forlán, with five goals each.

Statistical focus – teams with the most finals played:

Country	Finals	Won
Germany/West Germany	8	4
Brazil†	6	5
Italy	6	4
Argentina	6	3
France	4	2

†The 1950 World Cup in Brazil did not feature a proper final: four teams played a quadrangular tournament. Coincidentally, Brazil and Uruguay decided the competition in the final match.

Brazil 2014

* Few World Cup host countries were resolved as simply as Brazil 2014. In 2007, because the World Cup had not visited South America for 29 years, and during that time it would complete its tour of North America, Europe, Asia, and Africa (South Africa had already been confirmed as the 2010 host), FIFA determined that the 2014 tournament should be held in that continent. Surprisingly, only two nations submitted bids: Brazil and Colombia. But, a few months later, Colombia stepped back again, and Brazil's dream became a reality without a vote.

* Brazil's presence as the host country allowed South America to have six teams in the tournament: direct qualifiers Argentina, Colombia, Chile and Ecuador, Uruguay (after beating Jordan in an intercontinental play-off), and, of course, the home squad.

* In Europe, the biggest surprise was Bosnia and Herzegovina, who won their group and qualified for the first time since the split from the nations that made up the former Yugoslavia. Meanwhile, Portugal, who finished second in their group behind Russia, defeated Sweden in the play-offs thanks to a masterful performance by their star player, Cristiano Ronaldo. The forward scored four goals against Sweden: one in Lisbon and three in Stockholm.

* In CONCACAF, Mexico used four different coaches in five consecutive matches to secure their ticket to

Brazil. José Manuel de la Torre started the journey, but a home loss to Honduras ended his tenure. His replacement, Luis Fernando Tena, only managed one game, a defeat to the United States. Víctor Manuel Vucetich then led the team to a victory over Panama and a defeat to Costa Rica. Despite the setbacks, Mexico reached the intercontinental play-off against New Zealand – finishing fourth behind the United States, Costa Rica, and Honduras – although Mexican federation officials replaced Vucetich with Miguel Herrera, who secured their long-awaited spot in the World Cup with two wins.

* In Oceania, Tahiti fielded three brothers named Tehau: Jonathan and twins Alvin and Lorenzo. The squad also included a cousin of the boys, Teaonui Tehau. In the first continental round, the 'family' team crushed Samoa 10-1 and Vanuatu 4-1, but then fell apart against New Zealand.

* The Asian and African stages didn't leave much room for surprises. South Korea, Japan, Iran, and Australia advanced with great strength, as did Nigeria, Cameroon, Algeria, Ivory Coast, and Ghana.

* For this tournament, FIFA finally approved the incorporation of two technological elements: the vanishing spray that prevents the wall from moving forward when defending a free kick, and Hawk-Eye, a computer-controlled camera system that determines whether a ball has crossed the goal line.

* The opening match, between Brazil and Croatia, started with a surprise: left-back Marcelo opened the scoring 11 minutes in on 12 June at the São Paulo Arena. Of course, Marcelo's goal wasn't for his team, but for Croatia: Ivica Olić sent a low, powerful cross

from the left, and the ball, after rolling through many legs, bounced off the left-back's right foot and ended up in the net of Júlio César. Brazil ultimately won 3-1, but never before had a World Cup started with an own goal conceded.

* The following day, at the Fonte Nova Arena in Salvador, Spain and the Netherlands replayed the previous final. Spain, also back-to-back European Championship winners in 2008 and 2012, began their defence of their world title positively: in the 27th minute, Xabi Alonso opened the scoring with a penalty. But shortly afterwards, the crown began to wobble around their heads because two goals from Robin van Persie, two from Arjen Robben, and one from Stefan de Vrij gave the *Oranje* resounding revenge. Five days later, at the Maracanã in Rio de Janeiro, Chile dealt the 2010 champions the knockout blow with a resounding 2-0 victory.

* On 15 June, when France and Honduras faced each other at the Beira-Rio Stadium in Porto Alegre in Group E, goal-line technology was used for the first time. This instrument verified that a shot by French striker Karim Benzema had indeed crossed the line after bouncing off a post and goalkeeper Noel Valladares. This goal was the second in a resounding 3-0 French victory.

* Three days after Marcelo's own goal in the opener, Bosnia's Sead Kolašinac also achieved a dismal record: against Argentina at the Maracanã, he scored the fastest own goal in history, just two minutes and ten seconds after the kick-off (36 seconds faster than the goal scored by Paraguay's Carlos Gamarra in 2006). Like Marcelo, Kolašinac also suffered some bad

luck: a cross from Lionel Messi, headed by Marcos Rojo, deflected into the legs of the Bosnian defender, who was unable to avoid the impact. Thanks to this misfortune, Argentina won 2-1.

* The remarkable brotherly duel between Kevin-Prince and Jérôme Boateng was repeated on 21 June 2014, at the Castelão Stadium in Fortaleza. In this case, Germany and Ghana, 'brothered' by chance in Group G, drew 2-2, and the family members were together only during the first half as Jérôme was replaced at half-time by Shkodran Mustafi. The draw allowed Germany to finish first in their group, but Ghana were last and eliminated.

* Colombia, returning to the World Cup after a 16-year absence, won their group for the first time with three resounding victories against Greece, Ivory Coast, and Japan, and a memorable performance from their young star, James Rodríguez. Against Japan, goalkeeper Faryd Mondragón came on in the final minutes to replace David Ospina, becoming the oldest player to ever play in a World Cup at 43 years and three days old.

* When the draw for the group phase was held on 6 December 2013 in Salvador de Bahía, the football world took pity on Costa Rica as fate had sent the inexperienced Central American team to Group D alongside three world champions: England, Italy, and Uruguay. The press immediately dubbed it 'the group of death', and analysts racked their brains trying to predict which of the three former winners would be eliminated. However, Costa Rica put in a historic performance – beating Uruguay 3-1 and Italy 1-0, and drawing 0-0 with England after they had already

qualified – that not only left them in first place, but also sent the *Azzurri* and Three Lions home.

* 'In the group of death, the dead are others,' said Costa Rica captain Bryan Ruiz.

* With Costa Rica already qualified, Italy and Uruguay competed for the second and final spot at the Estadio das Dunas in Natal. In a match hotter than the Brazilian climate, which that day raised the thermometer to 33ºC, Mexican referee Marco Rodríguez sent off Italy's Claudio Marchisio for a violent foul. Ten minutes before the end, defender Giorgio Chiellini and forward Luis Suárez collided and went down together inside the Italian penalty area; the defender writhed in pain and complained of being bitten by Suárez. The referee hadn't noticed anything. Play continued, and a minute later, Diego Godín headed in the only goal, which secured the Uruguayans' qualification. After the match, FIFA reviewed the footage and suspended Suárez, who had a history of biting opponents, for nine international matches. It also banned the striker from 'any kind of activity related to football, whether administrative, sporting, or otherwise', for four months and imposed a fine equivalent to 100,000 Swiss francs.

* 'I know that a bite shocks many, but it's actually inoffensive,' wrote Luis Suárez in his autobiography, published months after being banned in Brazil.

* For the first time in the World Cup, two African teams, Nigeria and Algeria, qualified for the last 16 in the same tournament. Both were then eliminated at that stage, by France and Germany respectively.

* The woodwork saved Brazil from an early exit in the last 16 on their home turf. On 28 June, at the Estádio Mineirão in Belo Horizonte, they were level at 1-1 with Chile after almost two hours of play. However, with the clock ticking down to the final 20 seconds of extra time, Chilean striker Mauricio Pinilla could have wrapped things up: his right-footed shot beat goalkeeper Júlio César, cracked the crossbar, and went wide. In the penalty shoot-out, Brazil won 3-2 thanks to two saves from Júlio César, then Chile's final shot, by Gonzalo Jara, hit the post.

* Another heart-stopping penalty shoot-out occurred in the quarter-finals, after Costa Rica and the Netherlands played a goalless draw in a game filled with chances at both ends on 5 July at the Arena Fonte Nova in Salvador. Seconds before extra time expired, Dutch coach Louis van Gaal made a decisive change: he replaced goalkeeper Jasper Cillessen with one of the reserve keepers, Tim Krul, who had specifically studied the Central American players who had participated in Costa Rica's last-16 shoot-out against Greece. The move was a success, as Krul saved two shots and the Netherlands won 4-3.

* In the semi-final against Argentina at the Corinthians Arena in São Paulo, Louis van Gaal didn't repeat the goalkeeping change, and after two goalless hours the South Americans won the shoot-out. It was very curious that Jasper Cillessen didn't make any penalty saves, while Sergio Romero did save two, from Ron Vlaar and Wesley Sneijder. Why curious? Because Van Gaal stated in the post-match press conference that he had been the one who 'taught the Argentine goalkeeper how to save penalties' in

2007, when Romero played under the Dutchman at AZ Alkmaar.

* The other semi-final proved historic: at the Mineirão, Germany humiliated Brazil 7-1. Never before had a semi-finalist conceded so many goals (the closest had been in Uruguay 1930, where the United States and Yugoslavia were both beaten 6-1), and Brazil had never conceded so many in a World Cup match. What's more, they became the host nation with the most goals conceded in a World Cup, 14, after losing 3-0 to the Netherlands in the bronze medal match. Furthermore, German striker Miroslav Klose, who scored one goal that day and three in the tournament, overtook Ronaldo as the all-time top scorer in World Cup history, 16 to 15.

* In the final, Germany dispatched a tepid Argentina in extra time, with a solitary goal from Mario Götze. It became the most replayed World Cup Final: before Brazil 2014, they had played in the finals of Mexico 1986 (Argentina 3 West Germany 2) and Italy 1990 (West Germany 1 Argentina 0). Argentina and Germany also equalled the record for the most head-to-head matches held by Brazil and Sweden, with seven.

Statistical focus – matches with the most spectators, according to official statistics:

Match	Date	Stadium	Spectators
Brazil 1 Uruguay 2	16/07/1950	Maracanã	173,850†
Brazil 6 Spain 1	13/07/1950	Maracanã	152,772
Brazil 2 Yugoslavia 0	01/07/1950	Maracanã	142,429
Brazil 7 Sweden 1	09/07/1950	Maracanã	138,886
Argentina 3 Germany 2	29/06/1986	Azteca	114,600
Mexico 1 Paraguay 1	07/06/1986	Azteca	114,600

† The total attendance is estimated to have reached 200,000, due to the large number of people who entered the stadium without a ticket.

Russia 2018

* Russia was selected as the host of the 21st edition of the World Cup after beating two 'duos' of nations in the FIFA vote held on 2 December 2010, in Zurich: the eastern nation obtained 13 votes against 7 for the Spain–Portugal combination, and 2 for Belgium–Netherlands. The election sparked several allegations of corruption involving members of the FIFA board, but nothing was proven, and the tournament went ahead on time. Furthermore, the World Cup took place on two continents: the selection of Russia, a giant state that occupies a large portion of eastern Europe and almost a third of Asia, made this curious scenario possible.

* The CONMEBOL qualifying was led by the usual suspects, Brazil and Argentina, along with Uruguay and Colombia. But fifth place came with a small surprise: Peru, who hadn't participated in the World Cup since 1982 in Spain, reached the play-off spot and qualified after beating New Zealand. In the Andean nation, it is said that Pope Francis I had much to do with this 'miracle': in 2014, months before the World Cup in Brazil, Peruvian president Ollanta Humala took advantage of a visit to the Vatican to make an unusual proposal to His Holiness. 'Knowing your passion for football, I give you the Peruvian national team jersey and ask you, with the Heavenly Father, to help us so that Peru can once again be in the World Cup,' Humala told Francis I during

their meeting at the Holy See. At that time, Peru had made eight failed attempts to reach the top sporting tournament. The Pope's 'management' was successful because, to the delight of Humala and all his people, Peru qualified for Russia 2018, after 36 years away.

* The European qualifying phase produced several surprises: the Netherlands were eliminated after finishing third in Group A, led by France and Sweden. Group I was won by an astonishing performance by Iceland, who defeated Croatia, Ukraine and Turkey. In the second phase, Sweden eliminated four-time world champions Italy.

* In Africa, Egypt, Morocco, Nigeria, Senegal and Tunisia advanced without problems. In Asia, meanwhile, South Korea and Japan qualified easily, along with Iran and Saudi Arabia. Australia secured the fifth continental spot in the play-off against Honduras, who had eliminated the United States.

* In the CONCACAF zone, Panama qualified for a World Cup for the first time. They accompanied Mexico and Costa Rica, first and second in the standings, eliminating the United States and sending Honduras to the intercontinental play-off, which they lost to Australia.

* On 15 June, after Egypt lost 1-0 in their first group game, against Uruguay in Yekaterinburg, FIFA named Mohamed El-Shennawy as the best player of the match. As the Egypt goalkeeper was leaving the field, an official approached him to present him with the award, but El-Shennawy politely declined. Why? Because the prize was sponsored by the American brewery company Budweiser, and the player, faithful to the alcohol ban promoted by most

Muslim religious orders, refused to be photographed with a pint-shaped trophy decorated with the name of a beer. FIFA took note and modified the protocols for presenting the award: it accepted that a player could refuse it and removed Budweiser's name from the plaques broadcast on television when the winners were Morocco's Amine Harit, Senegal's Mbaye Niang, and Egypt's Mohamed Salah.

* In this edition, FIFA incorporated the now famous and widespread VAR, an acronym for Video Assistant Referee. Its first key intervention occurred on 16 June at the Kazan Arena, during the group match between France and Australia: Uruguayan referee Andrés Cunha was informed that France's Antoine Griezmann had been hit by defender Josh Ridson inside the Australian penalty area. Cunha, who had not noticed the infraction, watched the replay on a monitor and awarded the first World Cup penalty suggested by VAR, which Griezmann himself converted. The application of the assistant referee through cameras resulted in Russia 2018 registering the highest number of penalties in World Cup history, with 29, 11 more than Italy 1990, France 1998, and South Korea–Japan 2002, which, until then, held the record. Also on a regulatory level, FIFA authorised teams to make a fourth substitution, but only in the event of extra time.

* That same day, Iceland debuted in the World Cup with a very promising 1-1 draw against Argentina at Moscow's Otkrytie Arena. Goalkeeper Hannes Þór Halldórsson saved a penalty from Lionel Messi, helping to prevent the island team from losing.

* Also on 16 June, in Kaliningrad, Croatia easily defeated Nigeria 2-0. In the 86th minute, Croatian coach Zlatko Dalić ordered forward Nikola Kalinić to come on, but he refused, unhappy at not being a starter and annoyed at being called up for only a handful of minutes when the result was already decided. Dalić, furious at the indiscipline, expelled Kalinić from the squad and sent him home.

* Spain won Group B (tying Portugal on five points, albeit with a better goal difference) despite a serious institutional crisis: just two days before the opening match against Portugal, the president of the Royal Spanish Football Federation (RFEF), Luis Rubiales, announced the dismissal of coach Julen Lopetegui. The unusual decision was based on the fact that, just hours before the decision, Real Madrid had announced the hiring of Lopetegui and the payment of the corresponding release clause to the RFEF. Rubiales, offended by this attitude, dismissed Lopetegui and appointed former Real Madrid defender Fernando Hierro as his successor.

* 'The national team is the team of all Spaniards, and there are decisions we are obliged to make based on a course of action. Madrid is looking for a coach, and it is legitimate for them to seek their best interests. God forbid that I should give my opinion on Madrid's approach. But the Federation has an obligation: the coach is an employee of the Federation, and whoever handled the negotiations with him made a mistake,' said Luis Rubiales after the dismissal of Julen Lopetegui.

* An unprecedented event occurred in Group F: Germany were eliminated for the first time in the

World Cup group stage. The defending champions lost 1-0 to Mexico and 2-0 to South Korea. A victory over Sweden provided their only points and they had an early return home.

* On 25 June in Volgograd, Saudi Arabia defeated Egypt 2-1; Saudi goalkeeper Essam El-Hadary became the oldest player to appear in a World Cup match, playing at 45 years and 161 days. El-Hadary was 888 days older than his Colombian counterpart Faryd Mondragón, the previous record holder.

* In Group H, Japan and Senegal finished with four points, four goals scored and four conceded. They had also drawn 2-2 in Ekaterinburg. However, Japan advanced to the next round because they had collected four yellow cards, two fewer than Senegal. Thus, for the first time, a team qualified for the last 16 thanks to their 'fair play' behaviour.

* Argentina went through thanks to a hard-fought 2-1 victory over Nigeria on 26 June in Saint Petersburg. The goals were scored by Lionel Messi and Marcos Rojos, who, curiously, had both also scored against Nigeria in Brazil 2014. Several players have scored against the same opponents in two consecutive World Cups – Baltazar of Brazil against Mexico in 1950 and 1954; Martin Peters of England against West Germany in 1966 and 1970; Grzegorz Lato of Poland against Brazil in 1974 and 1978; and Miroslav Klose of Germany against Argentina in 2006 and 2010 – but only one pairing has repeated against the same opponent in the tournament's history: Messi and Rojo.

* On 27 June at the Ekaterinburg Arena, Mexico's Jesús Gallardo made his mark in the hall of records when

he was booked 13 seconds into the match against Sweden for striking his opponent Ola Toivonen.

* The last-16 matches produced several surprises: on 30 June, France defeated Argentina 4-3 at the Kazan Arena in an electrifying encounter that saw the scoring go back and forth, the Europeans coming out on top thanks to the scoring prowess of Kylian Mbappé. Another roller-coaster ride was Belgium v Japan on 2 July in Rostov: Japan were leading 2-0 until the 69th minute, but the Belgians fought back and scored three goals before the final whistle, to reach the quarter-finals.

* Both matches on 1 July were decided on penalties after ending 1-1: at Moscow's Luzhniki Stadium, Russia eliminated Spain 4-3 in the shoot-out; in Nizhny Novgorod, Croatia beat Denmark 3-2 thanks to their goalkeeper, Danijel Subašić, who saved three spot kicks. With Denmark's Kasper Schmeichel also saving two, this shoot-out became the one with the most shots stopped in World Cup history.

* On 3 July at Moscow's Otkrytie Arena, England's penalty shoot-out losing streak was broken when they beat Colombia 4-3, after another 1-1 draw. Andrés Uribe hitting the bar and a save by Jordan Pickford from Carlos Bacca sealed the result for England, who up to that point had lost each of their World Cup shoot-outs: against West Germany in 1990, Argentina in 1998, and Portugal in 2006.

* In the next round, France, Belgium, and England achieved resounding victories against Uruguay, Brazil, and Sweden, respectively. Croatia's journey to the semi-finals was more difficult, drawing 2-2 with Russia at Sochi's Fisht Stadium and having

to go all the way to penalties again. Another save from Danijel Subašić and a miss from Brazilian-born defender Mário Fernandes saw Croatia through. Thus, the 2018 World Cup became the fifth in which all the semi-finalists were European, following Italy 1934, England 1966, Spain 1982 and Germany 2006.

* France earned their place in the final thanks to a header from defender Samuel Umiti and the powerful hands of goalkeeper Hugo Lloris. Croatia, meanwhile, became the first team to reach the final after going through extra time in every stage: the last 16, the quarter-finals, and the semi-finals. However, they didn't need penalties to defeat England, as a left-footed shot from Mario Mandžukić, unstoppable for Jordan Pickford, settled the match in the 109th minute.

* France earned their second star after defeating Croatia 4-2 in the final on 15 July at the Luzhniki Stadium in Moscow. Backed by the versatility of the skilful Antoine Griezmann and the dizzying runs of Kylian Mbappé, they also had some help from their opponents: Mario Mandžukić scored one goal for his team, and an own goal in France's favour. Griezmann, Mbappé, and Paul Pogba completed the scoring. The golden coach, Didier Deschamps, who had already lifted the World Cup as a player in 1998, joined the select and small group of people to have completed the lap of honour as both players and coaches, which until then only included Brazil's Mário Zagallo and West Germany's Franz Beckenbauer.

* 'I don't want the medal because I didn't contribute during the tournament, I didn't share in the team's achievement,' said the unruly Croatian player Zlatko

Dalić, expelled from the squad after refusing to play against Nigeria in the first round, explaining his rejection of the silver medal he was entitled to.

Statistical focus – referees with the most World Cup matches officiated:

Referee	Country	Matches
Ravshan Irmatov	Uzbekistan	11 (2010, 2014, 2018)
Néstor Pitana	Argentina	9 (2014, 2018)
Joël Quiniou	France	8 (1986, 1990, 1994)
Benito Archundia	Mexico	8 (2006, 2010)
Jorge Larrionda	Uruguay	8 (2006, 2010)

Qatar 2022

* Qatar's selection as the host country for the 22nd World Cup took shape on the same day that Russia was designated for the 2018 tournament: 2 December 2010. The election of the minuscule country – which beat the United States, Japan, South Korea, and Australia in the voting – was highly controversial, as it had no football tradition or the infrastructure necessary to host such a major tournament. The Kingdom of Qatar became the smallest host state in World Cup history, with just 11,627 square kilometres (4,500 square miles). Only one of the eight stadiums used throughout the World Cup was fully built. Hotel capacity was overwhelmed, and many fans who travelled to follow their teams had to stay in neighbouring countries, such as Saudi Arabia, Bahrain, and the United Arab Emirates. But the main problem was related to the weather: in June and July, when the competition traditionally takes place, temperatures in Qatar often reach 50ºC. Therefore, FIFA moved the calendar to the end of November, the 'winter' season in that part of the world. Of course, this change in dates forced the rescheduling of domestic and continental tournaments, which had to be frozen until the end of the World Cup. Furthermore, this tournament – and its qualifying phase – had to endure some restrictions and changes due to the coronavirus pandemic, which severely affected the world's population.

QATAR 2022

* The most striking case in the qualifying was that of Italy. They once again missed out on a place in the finals, but in an unusual way: in the group stage, Italy had two penalties against Switzerland, one in the 0-0 draw in Basel and another in the 1-1 draw at the Olympic Stadium in Rome. Both were missed by Brazilian-born midfielder Jorginho. Just one would have been enough to secure the group and a direct ticket to the World Cup. But Italy, second behind Switzerland by just two points, advanced to the play-offs and were definitively eliminated from Qatar after losing 1-0 at the Renzo Barbera Stadium in Sicily to first-time qualifiers North Macedonia.

* In the South American group, Colombia missed out on the intercontinental play-offs by one point, behind Peru – who would later be eliminated by Australia on penalties. Colombia started off well, but went six games without scoring, which dashed their hopes.

* Brazil and Argentina, who qualified without losing a single match throughout the qualifying round, played a 'ghost game'. Their meeting on 5 September 2021, at the Corinthians Arena in São Paulo, lasted for just 316 seconds when it was interrupted by the local government. Officials from the National Health Surveillance Agency entered the field and stopped the match to arrest four visiting players – Emiliano Martínez, Emiliano Buendía, Cristian Romero and Giovani Lo Celso, all residents of England at the time – accused of violating the safety protocols established to combat the coronavirus pandemic. Venezuelan referee Jesús Valenzuela formally suspended the match, and months later, after the two teams' qualifications had been confirmed,

FIFA resolved the situation with a pair of fines. The fixture was never resumed, and its result is listed as 'cancelled'.

* Qatar's presence as the host nation allowed the Asian association to field six participating teams: the home squad, making their World Cup debut, along with Saudi Arabia, South Korea, Iran, Japan, and Australia, who qualified in the intercontinental play-off against Peru.

* The coronavirus pandemic affected the qualifying stage and prompted FIFA to adopt some measures for the finals: squads were allowed 26 players and five substitutions per 90 minutes, which could only be made in three 'windows'. An additional substitution was also allowed if knockout matches required extra time, and a seventh if a player suffered a head injury that could raise concerns of a concussion. In the final, France became the only team to make all seven available substitutions.

* Qatar 2022 was the scene of a very curious situation: 60 of the participant players were born in France. According to official records, 37 players of French origin represented Germany (1), Cameroon (8), Spain (1), Ghana (3), Morocco (3), Portugal (1), Qatar (1), Senegal (9), and Tunisia (10). In addition, another 23 were born in France and played in the blue shirt: the defending champions from Russia 2018 included three naturalised players in Eduardo Camavinga (born in Angola), Marcus Thuram (Italy), and Steve Mandanda (Zaire).

* In Group A, Qatar, the only debutants, had the worst performance of any host team in the World Cup: they lost all three of their matches, against Ecuador,

QATAR 2022

the Netherlands, and Senegal. They conceded seven goals and scored only one. Like South Africa in 2010, they were eliminated in the group stage, but unlike South Africa, they didn't earn a single point. Furthermore, Qatar fielded one of the most cosmopolitan squads in World Cup history, if not the most diverse: of their 26 players, ten were born outside the small Asian country, two were of Iraqi origin, two Sudanese, one Portuguese, one French, one Egyptian, one Bahraini, one Ghanaian, and one Algerian.

* On 21 November at the Khalifa International Stadium in Al Rayyan, England thrashed Iran 6-2 in Group B, in the longest group match in World Cup history: Brazilian referee Raphael Claus added 14 minutes to the first half and 13 to the second half, extending the playing time to 117 minutes. Eight days later, England faced Wales in the first British World Cup duel in almost 100 years. The Three Lions won 3-0, with two goals from Marcus Rashford and one from Phil Foden.

* Group C began with a surprising result. On 22 November, at Lusail Stadium, Argentina opened the scoring in the tenth minute through a penalty from Lionel Messi. The first half ended 1-0, despite the Argentines squandering several chances. In the second half, Saudi Arabia turned the score around and eventually won 2-1, with goals from Saleh Al-Shehri and Salem Al-Dawsari. Argentina had to win their two remaining matches, against Mexico and Poland, to advance. They achieved this with 2-0 victories, backed by the brilliance of Lionel Messi and a team that began to improve with each game.

* On 24 November at the Al Janoub Stadium in Al Wakrah, an unprecedented event occurred: a player scored a goal against his country of birth. Breel Embolo, born in Cameroon but a Swiss national, scored for Switzerland against the Indomitable Lions in the opening round of Group G.

* That feat was repeated six days later, at the Education City Stadium in Al Rayyan when Tunisia defeated France 1-0 with a goal scored by Wahbi Khazri, born in Corsica, a French island in the Mediterranean. This match had an additional curiosity: Tunisia had more players born in France (six) than in Tunisia itself (five). This defeat did not prevent the defending champions from qualifying for the second round, finishing first in their group.

* Also on 24 November, at Stadium 974 in Doha, Portugal defeated Ghana 3-2 in Group H. The first goal for Portugal came from striker Cristiano Ronaldo, who became the only player to score in five consecutive World Cups: 2006, 2010, 2014, 2018 and 2022.

* Japan's performance was extraordinary: in a very close and difficult Group E, they defeated Germany and Spain by the same score, 2-1, and qualified for the next round. However, they lost 1-0 to Costa Rica. Spain also went through thanks to their biggest win in World Cup history: 7-0 against Costa Rica. The Germans were once again eliminated in the first round.

* On 1 December, at the Al Bayt de Jor Coliseum, France's Stéphanie Frappart became the first woman to referee a match at the men's World Cup: Costa Rica v Germany, in Group E of the initial phase.

Frappart was accompanied by two other women as her assistants, Brazil's Neuza Back and Mexico's Karen Díaz. Germany won 4-2.

* For the first time, two African teams, Morocco and Senegal, and three 'Asian' teams – Japan, South Korea, and Australia, which belongs to another continent but is federationally affiliated with the Asian association – reached the last 16.

* On 5 December at Al Janoub Stadium in Al Wakrah, Croatian goalkeeper Dominik Livaković repeated his predecessor Danijel Subašić's feat against Denmark in Russia: he saved three penalties, from Japan's Takumi Minamino, Kaoru Mitoma, and Maya Yoshida. Croatia won the shoot-out after a tough match had ended 1-1.

* The following day in Rayyan, after two goalless hours, Moroccan goalkeeper Yassine Bounou became a hero by saving from Spaniards Carlos Soler and Sergio Busquets. When Pablo Sarabia then hit the post, Morocco won the penalty shoot-out 3-0 and reached the quarter-finals.

* Dominik Livaković was once again a hero on 9 December in Rayyan, where Croatia faced Brazil. Livaković made two exceptional saves during the 90 minutes, which ended goalless. In the final moments of extra time, with the score at 1-1 after goals by Neymar and Bruno Petković, the goalkeeper thwarted a left-footed shot from Casemiro that seemed set to seal the victory for the South Americans. In the shoot-out, Livaković blocked Rodrygo's shot, and Croatia went through 4-2 after Marquinhos's shot was deflected on to the post by the extraordinary stopper. Croatia qualified for the semi-finals, and

Brazil said goodbye with a record: they were the only team to use all 26 squad players, in just five matches.

* That same day in Lusail, Argentina and the Netherlands put on a thrilling display. Right-back Nahuel Molina broke the deadlock in the first half, and Lionel Messi made it 2-0 in the 73rd minute. It seemed like a comfortable victory for Argentina, but giant striker Wout Weghorst came on to help his team come back and equalise. After a goalless extra time, but with plenty of violent action – Spanish referee Antonio Mateu Lahoz showed 16 yellow cards – South American goalkeeper Emiliano Martínez gave his team the victory by saving penalties from Virgil van Dijk and Steven Berghuis. Successful spot kicks from Messi, Leandro Paredes, Gonzalo Montiel and Lautaro Martínez sealed the victory for Lionel Scaloni's team.

* One day later, at Doha's Al Thumama Stadium, Morocco achieved what no African team had done up to that point in World Cup history by qualifying for the semi-finals. The Atlas Lions, led by coach Walid Regragui – a Moroccan who was born in France, like many of his players – defeated Portugal 1-0 thanks to a header from Youssef En-Nesyri in the 42nd minute. Two stunning saves from Yassine Bounou, a shot off the crossbar, and some bad misses from the Portuguese contributed to the Moroccans' remarkable result.

* Both semi-finals were resolved fairly simply, for Argentina and France. Argentina thrashed Croatia 3-0, with a penalty from Lionel Messi and two goals from their new young star, Julián Álvarez. France, meanwhile, had no trouble defeating Morocco 2-0,

with goals from Théo Hernández and Randal Kolo Muani. Morocco were left without a medal because, in the play-off for third place, they lost 2-1 to Croatia.

* On 18 December in Lusail, the most thrilling and dramatic final in World Cup history took place between Argentina and France. In the first half, Argentina took a 2-0 lead thanks to another penalty from Lionel Messi and an outstanding team move that Ángel Di María finished off with tremendous skill. In the second half they went closer to a third goal than France did to get on the scoresheet, but just ten minutes from time Didier Deschamps' players pulled it back with a burst from Kylian Mbappé: his first, in the 80th minute, was a penalty, and a minute later his exceptional volley beat Emiliano Martínez and found the back of the net. In extra time, Messi sent a rebound off goalkeeper Hugo Lloris over the line, but another penalty converted by Mbappé levelled the score once again. Mbappé also tied the record held by England's Geoff Hurst since 1966 by scoring a hat-trick in the World Cup Final. France could have won it in the third minute of added time, when a long ball left Randal Kolo Muani alone against Martínez: the forward unleashed a powerful right-footed shot that *Dibu* parried with his left foot. The final ended 3-3, a score that was enough to establish Qatar 2022 as the World Cup with the most goals, 172, and the thrilling match was decided from the penalty spot. Argentina earned their third star thanks to the success of Messi, Dybala, Paredes and Montiel. Martínez, the hero of the day, saved Kingsley Coman's shot, while Aurélien Tchouaméni sent his wide.

* Lionel Messi broke several records in Qatar: in addition to equalling several players who have played in five editions, he became the player with the most appearances (26 games, between the 2006, 2010, 2014, 2018, and 2022 tournaments) and the most minutes played (2,316). He also reached the most penalties taken (excluding shoot-outs), with six: one in 2018 and five in 2022.

* 'Look at her! She's beautiful! Do you know how much I'm going to kiss her? I wanted her so much! We suffered a lot, but we got her,' said Lionel Messi, hugging the World Cup, on the Argentine television channel TyC Sports.

Statistical focus – World Cups with the highest total attendances:

Tournament	Attendees	Matches
USA 1994	3,587,538	52
Brazil 2014	3,429,873	64
Qatar 2022	3,404,252	64
Germany 2006	3,359,439	64
South Africa 2010	3,178,856	64